Common Core Lessons
Reading Informational Text
Grade 2

Writing: Barbara Allman
Editorial Development: Marti Beeck
Lisa Vitarisi Mathews
Copy Editing: Anna Pelligra
Art Direction: Cheryl Puckett
Art Coordination: Kathy Kopp
Cover Design: Yuki Meyer
Cover Illustration: Chris Vallo
Illustration: Ruth Flanigan
Design/Production: Marcia Smith
Jessica Onken

EMC 3202

Helping Children Learn

Visit
teaching-standards.com
to view a correlation
of this book.
This is a free service.

Correlated to State and Common Core State Standards

Congratulations on your purchase of some of the finest teaching materials in the world.

Photocopying the pages in this book is permitted for <u>single-classroom use only</u>. Making photocopies for additional classes or schools is prohibited.

For information about other Evan-Moor products, call 1-800-777-4362, fax 1-800-777-4332, or visit our Web site, www.evan-moor.com. Entire contents © 2014 EVAN-MOOR CORP. 18 Lower Ragsdale Drive, Monterey, CA 93940-5746. Printed in USA.

CPSIA: Printed by McNaughton & Gunn, Saline, MI USA. [9/2014]

Contents

Introduction

What's in Every Unit? 4
Correlations: *Common Core State Standards* 6
Correlations: *Texas Essential Knowledge and Skills* 8
Overview of Articles and Student Objectives 9
Student Record Sheet 10
Small-Group Record Sheet 11

Units

Science

LEVEL
- **I** Baby Blue Whale 12
  Text Structure: Question and Answer
- **L** Big Machines 22
  Text Structure: Main Idea and Details

Geography

LEVEL
- **K** Big Island Map 32
  Text Structure: Cause and Effect

Social Studies

LEVEL
- **I** TOMS Shoes 42
  Text Structure: Main Idea and Details
- **L** Rosa Parks Rides the Bus 52
  Text Structure: Compare and Contrast
- **M** What Does Congress Do? 62
  Text Structure: Time Order

Biography

LEVEL
- **J** Ben Franklin and the Glass Harmonica 72
  Text Structure: Time Order
- **K** Thank You, Sarah Josepha Hale 82
  Text Structure: Time Order

How-to

LEVEL
- **H** Fun with Magnets 92
  Text Structure: Cause and Effect

Technical

LEVEL
- **M** Help Wanted: Earth Engineer 102
  Text Structure: Compare and Contrast

What's in Every Unit?

Teacher resource pages are provided for lesson preparation and instructional guidance.

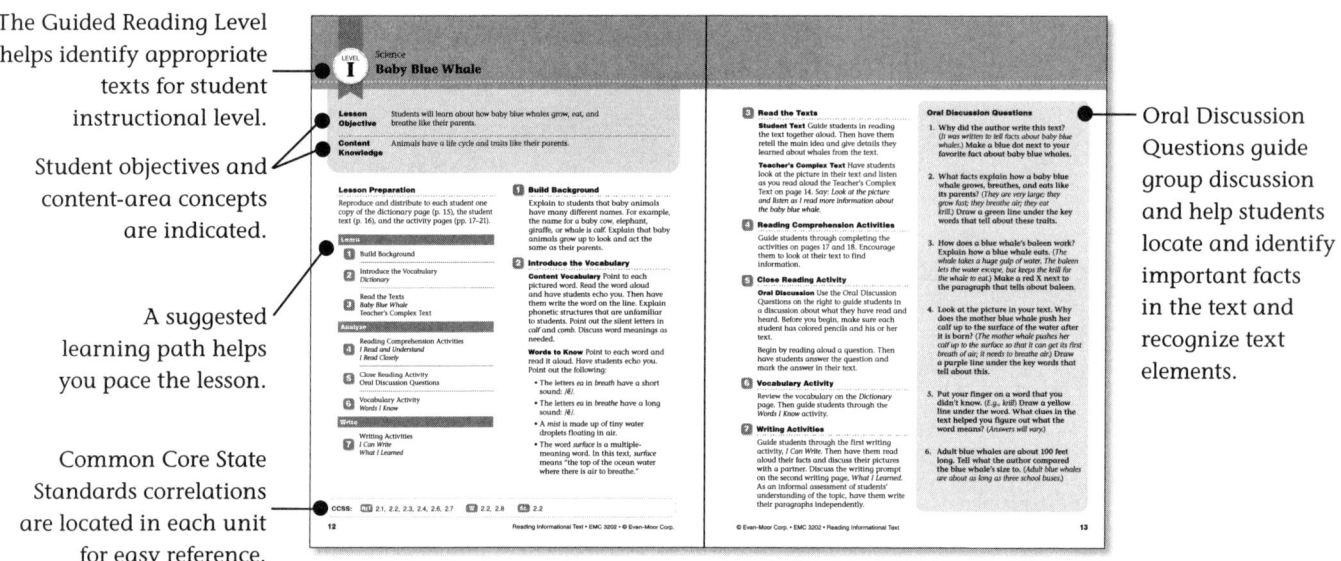

The Guided Reading Level helps identify appropriate texts for student instructional level.

Student objectives and content-area concepts are indicated.

A suggested learning path helps you pace the lesson.

Common Core State Standards correlations are located in each unit for easy reference.

Oral Discussion Questions guide group discussion and help students locate and identify important facts in the text and recognize text elements.

Students read one-page nonfiction texts about a variety of grade-level topics. Students listen to the Teacher's Complex Text read aloud, featuring the same topic.

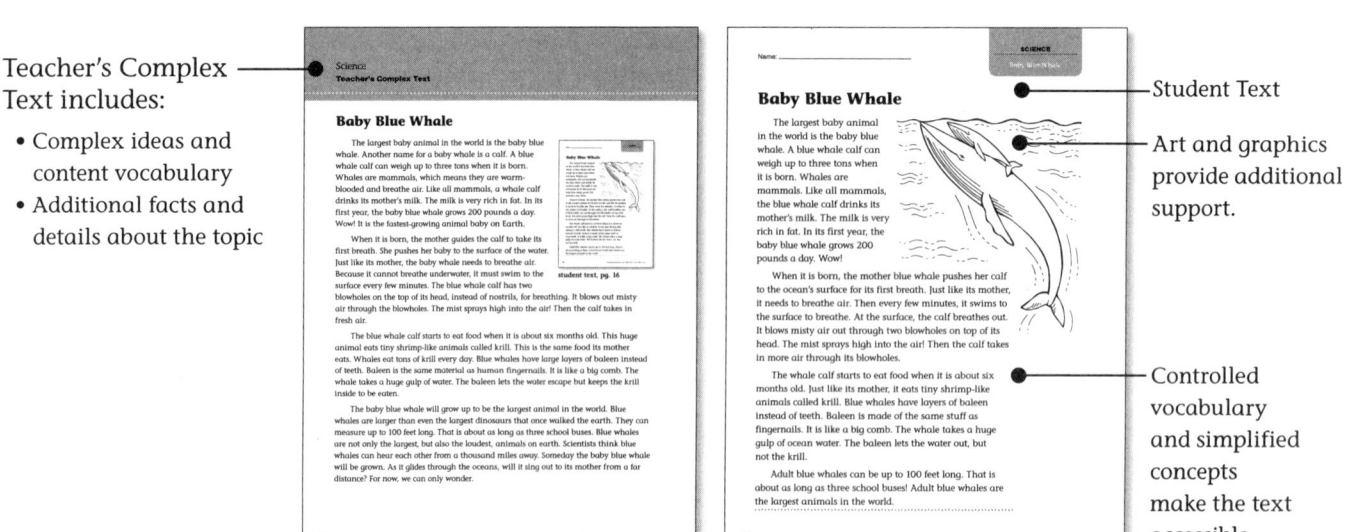

Teacher's Complex Text includes:
- Complex ideas and content vocabulary
- Additional facts and details about the topic

Student Text

Art and graphics provide additional support.

Controlled vocabulary and simplified concepts make the text accessible.

4   Reading Informational Text • EMC 3202 • © Evan-Moor Corp.

Student pages provide support for understanding the vocabulary and concepts in the text.

Dictionary

A picture dictionary page provides visual information for understanding of content vocabulary. A Words to Know list offers an opportunity for additional practice of vocabulary to be introduced prior to reading the nonfiction text.

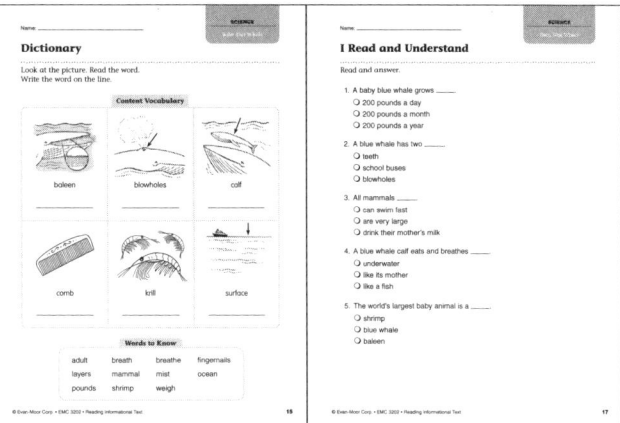

I Read and Understand

A reading comprehension activity asks students to answer questions about the nonfiction text, prompting them to examine it closely, and provides an informal assessment of students' understanding.

I Read Closely

A close reading activity presents students with pictures and sentences that ask them to connect text meaning and picture meaning.

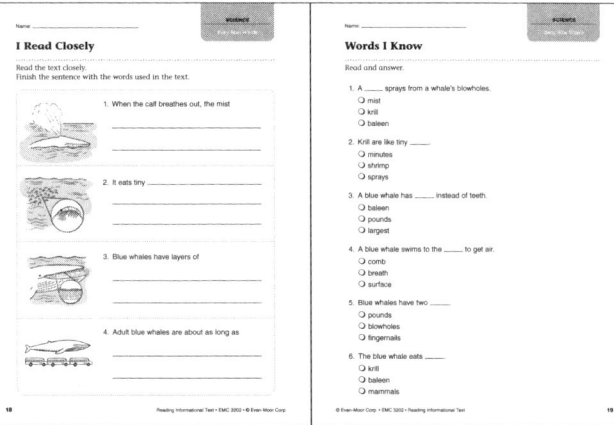

Words I Know

A vocabulary activity provides students another opportunity to interact with key words from the text and apply them in a similar context.

I Can Write

A scaffolded writing activity asks students to organize and summarize what they have read in the nonfiction text. This activity can be used as a prewriting activity for What I Learned on the following page.

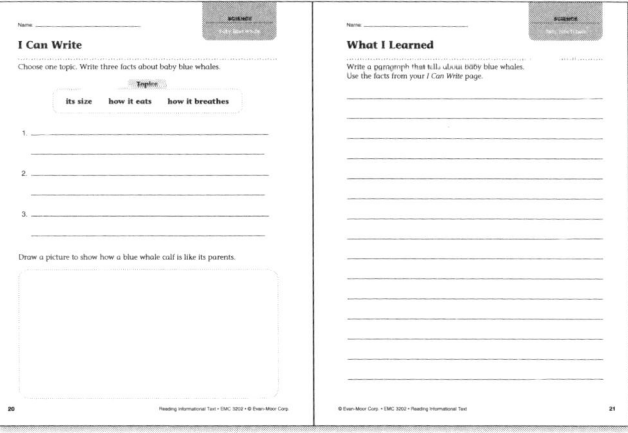

What I Learned

The unit culminates with a text-based writing assignment. Students will synthesize the information presented in the text to show their understanding.

Student Record Sheet

A reproducible record sheet provides a place to track individual student progress through all units.

Small-Group Record Sheet

A reproducible sheet provides a place to keep track of small-group progress.

© Evan-Moor Corp. • EMC 3202 • Reading Informational Text

Correlations
Common Core State Standards

RIT Reading Standards for Informational Text, Grade 2	Units				
	Baby Blue Whale	Big Machines	Big Island Map	TOMS Shoes	Rosa Parks Rides the Bus
Key Ideas and Details					
2.1 Ask and answer such questions as *who*, *what*, *where*, *when*, *why*, and *how* to demonstrate understanding of key details in a text.	●	●	●	●	●
2.2 Identify the main topic of a multiparagraph text as well as the focus of specific paragraphs within the text.	●	●	●	●	●
2.3 Describe the connection between a series of historical events, scientific ideas or concepts, or steps in technical procedures in a text.	●	●	●	●	●
Craft and Structure					
2.4 Determine the meaning of words and phrases in a text relevant to a grade 2 topic or subject area.	●	●	●	●	●
2.6 Identify the main purpose of a text, including what the author wants to answer, explain, or describe.	●	●	●	●	●
Integration of Knowledge and Ideas					
2.7 Explain how specific images (e.g., a diagram showing how a machine works) contribute to and clarify a text.	●	●	●		●

W Writing Standards for Grade 2					
Text Types and Purposes					
2.2 Write informative/explanatory texts in which they introduce a topic, use facts and definitions to develop points, and provide a concluding statement or section.	●	●	●	●	●
Research to Build and Present Knowledge					
2.8 Recall information from experiences or gather information from provided sources to answer a question.	●	●	●	●	●

SL Speaking and Listening Standards for Grade 2					
Comprehension and Collaboration					
2.2 Recount or describe key ideas or details from a text read aloud or information presented orally or through other media.	●	●	●	●	●

Units						
What Does Congress Do?	Ben Franklin and the Glass Harmonica	Thank You, Sarah Josepha Hale	Fun with Magnets	Help Wanted: Earth Engineer	**RIT**	**Reading Standards for Informational Text, Grade 2**
						**Key Ideas and Details**
●	●	●	●	●		2.1 Ask and answer such questions as *who, what, where, when, why,* and *how* to demonstrate understanding of key details in a text.
●	●	●	●	●		2.2 Identify the main topic of a multiparagraph text as well as the focus of specific paragraphs within the text.
●	●	●	●	●		2.3 Describe the connection between a series of historical events, scientific ideas or concepts, or steps in technical procedures in a text.
						Craft and Structure
●	●	●	●	●		2.4 Determine the meaning of words and phrases in a text relevant to a grade 2 topic or subject area.
●	●	●	●	●		2.6 Identify the main purpose of a text, including what the author wants to answer, explain, or describe.
						Integration of Knowledge and Ideas
●	●	●	●	●		2.7 Explain how specific images (e.g., a diagram showing how a machine works) contribute to and clarify a text.
					W	**Writing Standards for Grade 2**
						Text Types and Purposes
●	●	●	●	●		2.2 Write informative/explanatory texts in which they introduce a topic, use facts and definitions to develop points, and provide a concluding statement or section.
						Research to Build and Present Knowledge
●	●	●	●	●		2.8 Recall information from experiences or gather information from provided sources to answer a question.
					SL	**Speaking and Listening Standards for Grade 2**
						Comprehension and Collaboration
●	●	●	●	●		2.2 Recount or describe key ideas or details from a text read aloud or information presented orally or through other media.

Correlations
Texas Essential Knowledge and Skills

Units

English Language Arts and Reading Standards for Informational Text, Grade 2	Baby Blue Whale	Big Machines	Big Island Map	TOMS Shoes	Rosa Parks Rides the Bus	What Does Congress Do?	Ben Franklin and the Glass Harmonica	Thank You, Sarah Josepha Hale	Fun with Magnets	Help Wanted: Earth Engineer
(13) Reading/Comprehension of Informational Text/Culture and History. Students analyze, make inferences and draw conclusions about the author's purpose in cultural, historical, and contemporary contexts, and provide evidence from the text to support their understanding. Students are expected to identify the topic and explain the author's purpose in writing the text.				●		●	●	●		
(14) Reading/Comprehension of Informational Text/Expository Text. Students analyze, make inferences and draw conclusions about expository text, and provide evidence from text to support their understanding. Students are expected to:										
(A) identify the main idea in a text and distinguish it from the topic.	●	●	●	●	●	●	●	●	●	●
(B) locate the facts that are clearly stated in a text.	●	●	●	●	●	●	●	●	●	●
(C) describe the order of events or ideas in a text.	●	●	●	●	●	●	●	●	●	●
(D) use text features (e.g., table of contents, index, headings) to locate specific information in text.		●	●			●			●	
(15) Reading/Comprehension of Informational Text/Procedural Text. Students understand how to glean and use information in procedural texts and documents. Students are expected to:										
(A) follow written multi-step directions.	●	●	●	●	●	●	●	●	●	●
(B) use common graphic features to assist in the interpretation of text (e.g., captions, illustrations).	●	●	●	●	●	●	●	●	●	●
(19) Writing/Expository and Procedural Texts. Students write expository and procedural or work-related texts to communicate ideas and information to specific audiences for specific purposes. Students are expected to:										
(C) write brief comments on literary or informational texts.	●	●	●	●	●	●	●	●	●	●

Overview of Articles and Student Objectives

Title	Level	Content Area	Student Objective
Fun with Magnets	H	How-to (Science)	Students will learn that magnetic forces can pull objects that contain iron or steel.
Baby Blue Whale	I	Science	Students will learn about how baby blue whales grow, eat, and breathe like their parents.
TOMS Shoes	I	Social Studies (Economics)	Students will learn about a company, TOMS Shoes, and how it helps children.
Ben Franklin and the Glass Harmonica	J	Biography (Science/Arts)	Students will learn how Benjamin Franklin was not only a leader, but also a person of many other talents. They will become familiar with one of his inventions: the glass harmonica.
Big Island Map	K	Social Studies (Geography)	Students will learn about some physical features of the island of Hawaii on a grid map.
Thank You, Sarah Josepha Hale	K	Biography (Social Studies)	Students will learn how Sarah Josepha Hale helped to influence the creation of a Thanksgiving Day national holiday.
Big Machines	L	Science	Students will learn about six different big machines and the kinds of work they do.
Rosa Parks Rides the Bus	L	Social Studies	Students will learn about Rosa Parks wanting to be treated fairly. Students will understand how her experience started a movement that helped improve equality.
What Does Congress Do?	M	Social Studies	Students will learn what the United States Congress is and how Congress makes new laws.
Help Wanted: Earth Engineer	M	Technical (Social Studies)	Students will learn that geology is the study of Earth's soil and rocks. They will also learn that an earth engineer works to take care of the earth and keep people safe.

Reading Informational Text
Student Record Sheet

Grade 2

Student: _____

Number of correct answers/total possible	I Read and Understand	I Read Closely	Words I Know	I Can Write	What I Learned
I Unit 1: Baby Blue Whale					
L Unit 2: Big Machines					
K Unit 3: Big Island Map					
I Unit 4: TOMS Shoes					
L Unit 5: Rosa Parks Rides the Bus					
M Unit 6: What Does Congress Do?					
J Unit 7: Ben Franklin and the Glass Harmonica					
K Unit 8: Thank You, Sarah Josepha Hale					
H Unit 9: Fun with Magnets					
M Unit 10: Help Wanted: Earth Engineer					

Reading Informational Text
Small-Group Record Sheet

Grade 2

Group _____

Date _____ Unit Name _____

Write student names and comments about students' performance.

Student	Comments

Science
Baby Blue Whale

LEVEL I

Lesson Objective Students will learn about how baby blue whales grow, eat, and breathe like their parents.

Content Knowledge Animals have a life cycle and traits like their parents.

Lesson Preparation

Reproduce and distribute to each student one copy of the dictionary page (p. 15), the student text (p. 16), and the activity pages (pp. 17–21).

Learn

1. Build Background
2. Introduce the Vocabulary
   Dictionary
3. Read the Texts
   Baby Blue Whale
   Teacher's Complex Text

Analyze

4. Reading Comprehension Activities
   I Read and Understand
   I Read Closely
5. Close Reading Activity
   Oral Discussion Questions
6. Vocabulary Activity
   Words I Know

Write

7. Writing Activities
   I Can Write
   What I Learned

1 Build Background

Explain to students that baby animals have many different names. For example, the name for a baby cow, elephant, giraffe, or whale is *calf*. Explain that baby animals grow up to look and act the same as their parents.

2 Introduce the Vocabulary

Content Vocabulary Point to each pictured word. Read the word aloud and have students echo you. Then have them write the word on the line. Explain phonetic structures that are unfamiliar to students. Point out the silent letters in *calf* and *comb*. Discuss word meanings as needed.

Words to Know Point to each word and read it aloud. Have students echo you. Point out the following:

- The letters *ea* in *breath* have a short sound: /ĕ/.
- The letters *ea* in *breathe* have a long sound: /ē/.
- A *mist* is made up of tiny water droplets floating in air.
- The word *surface* is a multiple-meaning word. In this text, *surface* means "the top of the ocean water where there is air to breathe."

CCSS: RIT 2.1, 2.2, 2.3, 2.4, 2.6, 2.7   W 2.2, 2.8   SL 2.2

3 Read the Texts

Student Text Guide students in reading the text together aloud. Then have them retell the main idea and give details they learned about whales from the text.

Teacher's Complex Text Have students look at the picture in their text and listen as you read aloud the Teacher's Complex Text on page 14. Say: *Look at the picture and listen as I read more information about the baby blue whale.*

4 Reading Comprehension Activities

Guide students through completing the activities on pages 17 and 18. Encourage them to look at their text to find information.

5 Close Reading Activity

Oral Discussion Use the Oral Discussion Questions on the right to guide students in a discussion about what they have read and heard. Before you begin, make sure each student has colored pencils and his or her text.

Begin by reading aloud a question. Then have students answer the question and mark the answer in their text.

6 Vocabulary Activity

Review the vocabulary on the *Dictionary* page. Then guide students through the *Words I Know* activity.

7 Writing Activities

Guide students through the first writing activity, *I Can Write*. Then have them read aloud their facts and discuss their pictures with a partner. Discuss the writing prompt on the second writing page, *What I Learned*. As an informal assessment of students' understanding of the topic, have them write their paragraphs independently.

Oral Discussion Questions

1. Why did the author write this text? (*It was written to tell facts about baby blue whales.*) Make a blue dot next to your favorite fact about baby blue whales.

2. What facts explain how a baby blue whale grows, breathes, and eats like its parents? (*They are very large; they grow fast; they breathe air; they eat krill.*) Draw a green line under the key words that tell about these traits.

3. How does a blue whale's baleen work? Explain how a blue whale eats. (*The whale takes a huge gulp of water. The baleen lets the water escape, but keeps the krill for the whale to eat.*) Make a red X next to the paragraph that tells about baleen.

4. Look at the picture in your text. Why does the mother blue whale push her calf up to the surface of the water after it is born? (*The mother whale pushes her calf up to the surface so that it can get its first breath of air; it needs to breathe air.*) Draw a purple line under the key words that tell about this.

5. Put your finger on a word that you didn't know. (*E.g., krill*) Draw a yellow line under the word. What clues in the text helped you figure out what the word means? (*Answers will vary.*)

6. Adult blue whales are about 100 feet long. Tell what the author compared the blue whale's size to. (*Adult blue whales are about as long as three school buses.*)

Science
Teacher's Complex Text

Baby Blue Whale

The largest baby animal in the world is the baby blue whale. Another name for a baby whale is a calf. A blue whale calf can weigh up to three tons when it is born. Whales are mammals, which means they are warm-blooded and breathe air. Like all mammals, a whale calf drinks its mother's milk. The milk is very rich in fat. In its first year, the baby blue whale grows 200 pounds a day. Wow! It is the fastest-growing animal baby on Earth.

When it is born, the mother guides the calf to take its first breath. She pushes her baby to the surface of the water. Just like its mother, the baby whale needs to breathe air. Because it cannot breathe underwater, it must swim to the surface every few minutes. The blue whale calf has two blowholes on the top of its head, instead of nostrils, for breathing. It blows out misty air through the blowholes. The mist sprays high into the air! Then the calf takes in fresh air.

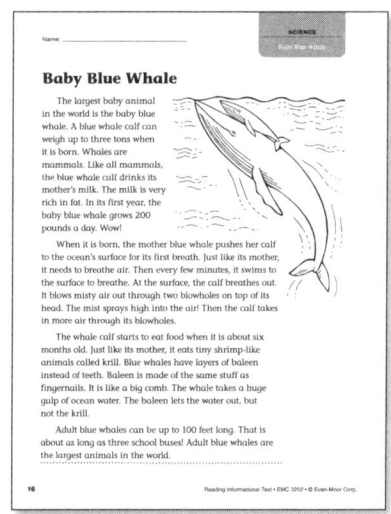

student text, pg. 16

The blue whale calf starts to eat food when it is about six months old. This huge animal eats tiny shrimp-like animals called krill. This is the same food its mother eats. Whales eat tons of krill every day. Blue whales have large layers of baleen instead of teeth. Baleen is the same material as human fingernails. It is like a big comb. The whale takes a huge gulp of water. The baleen lets the water escape but keeps the krill inside to be eaten.

The baby blue whale will grow up to be the largest animal in the world. Blue whales are larger than even the largest dinosaurs that once walked the earth. They can measure up to 100 feet long. That is about as long as three school buses. Blue whales are not only the largest, but also the loudest, animals on earth. Scientists think blue whales can hear each other from a thousand miles away. Someday the baby blue whale will be grown. As it glides through the oceans, will it sing out to its mother from a far distance? For now, we can only wonder.

Name: _____

SCIENCE

Baby Blue Whale

Dictionary

Look at the picture. Read the word.
Write the word on the line.

Content Vocabulary

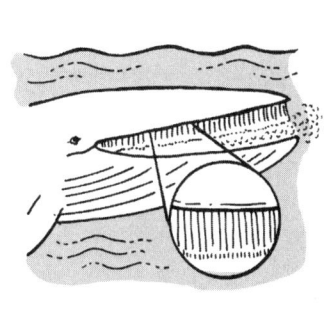

baleen

_____

blowholes

_____

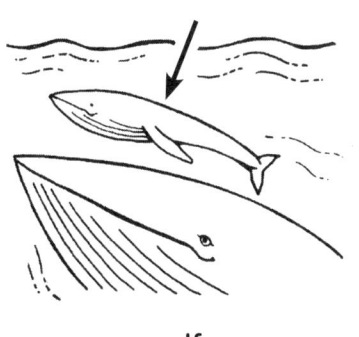

calf

_____

comb

_____

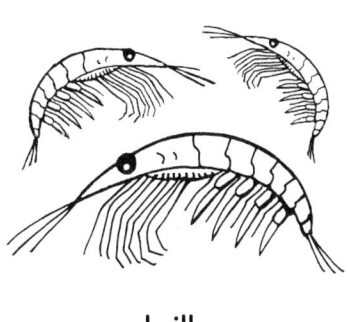

krill

_____

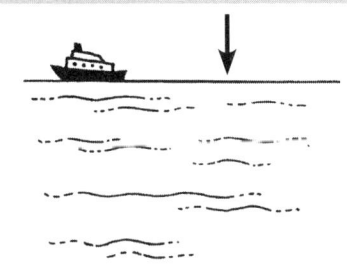

surface

_____

Words to Know

adult	breath	breathe	fingernails
layers	mammal	mist	ocean
pounds	shrimp	weigh	

Baby Blue Whale

The largest baby animal in the world is the baby blue whale. A blue whale calf can weigh up to three tons when it is born. Whales are mammals. Like all mammals, the blue whale calf drinks its mother's milk. The milk is very rich in fat. In its first year, the baby blue whale grows 200 pounds a day. Wow!

When it is born, the mother blue whale pushes her calf to the ocean's surface for its first breath. Just like its mother, it needs to breathe air. Then every few minutes, it swims to the surface to breathe. At the surface, the calf breathes out. It blows misty air out through two blowholes on top of its head. The mist sprays high into the air! Then the calf takes in more air through its blowholes.

The whale calf starts to eat food when it is about six months old. Just like its mother, it eats tiny shrimp-like animals called krill. Blue whales have layers of baleen instead of teeth. Baleen is made of the same stuff as fingernails. It is like a big comb. The whale takes a huge gulp of ocean water. The baleen lets the water out, but not the krill.

Adult blue whales can be up to 100 feet long. That is about as long as three school buses! Adult blue whales are the largest animals in the world.

Name: _____

SCIENCE

Baby Blue Whale

I Read and Understand

Read and answer.

1. A baby blue whale grows _____.
   - ○ 200 pounds a day
   - ○ 200 pounds a month
   - ○ 200 pounds a year

2. A blue whale has two _____.
   - ○ teeth
   - ○ school buses
   - ○ blowholes

3. All mammals _____.
   - ○ can swim fast
   - ○ are very large
   - ○ drink their mother's milk

4. A blue whale calf eats and breathes _____.
   - ○ underwater
   - ○ like its mother
   - ○ like a fish

5. The world's largest baby animal is a _____.
   - ○ shrimp
   - ○ blue whale
   - ○ baleen

Name: _____

I Read Closely

SCIENCE

Baby Blue Whale

Read the text closely.
Finish the sentence with the words used in the text.

1. When the calf breathes out, the mist

   _____

   _____

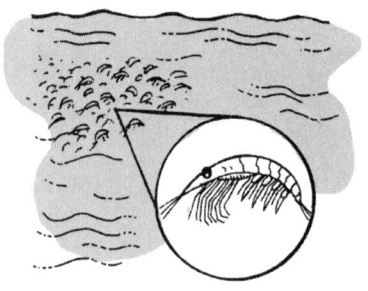
2. It eats tiny _____

   _____

   _____

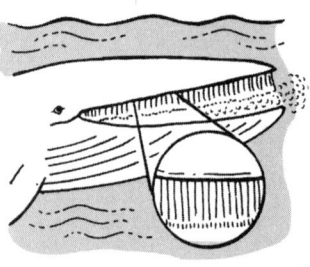
3. Blue whales have layers of

   _____

   _____

4. Adult blue whales are about as long as

   _____

   _____

Name: _____

SCIENCE

Baby Blue Whale

Words I Know

Read and answer.

1. A _____ sprays from a whale's blowholes.
   - ○ mist
   - ○ krill
   - ○ baleen

2. Krill are like tiny _____.
   - ○ minutes
   - ○ shrimp
   - ○ sprays

3. A blue whale has _____ instead of teeth.
   - ○ baleen
   - ○ pounds
   - ○ largest

4. A blue whale swims to the _____ to get air.
   - ○ comb
   - ○ breath
   - ○ surface

5. Blue whales have two _____.
   - ○ pounds
   - ○ blowholes
   - ○ fingernails

6. The blue whale eats _____.
   - ○ krill
   - ○ baleen
   - ○ mammals

© Evan-Moor Corp. • EMC 3202 • Reading Informational Text

Name: _____

I Can Write

Choose one topic. Write three facts about baby blue whales.

Topics

its size how it eats how it breathes

1. _____
   _____

2. _____
   _____

3. _____
   _____

Draw a picture to show how a blue whale calf is like its parents.

Name: _____

SCIENCE

Baby Blue Whale

What I Learned

Write a paragraph that tells about baby blue whales. Use the facts from your *I Can Write* page.

_____
_____
_____
_____
_____
_____
_____
_____
_____
_____
_____
_____
_____

Science
Big Machines

Lesson Objective Students will learn about six different big machines and the kinds of work they do.

Content Knowledge A machine does work, and there are different machines for different jobs.

Lesson Preparation

Reproduce and distribute to each student one copy of the dictionary page (p. 25), the student text (p. 26), and the activity pages (pp. 27–31).

Learn

1. Build Background
2. Introduce the Vocabulary
   Dictionary
3. Read the Texts
   Big Machines
   Teacher's Complex Text

Analyze

4. Reading Comprehension Activities
   I Read and Understand
   I Read Closely
5. Close Reading Activity
   Oral Discussion Questions
6. Vocabulary Activity
   Words I Know

Write

7. Writing Activities
   I Can Write
   What I Learned

1 Build Background

Explain to students that a machine is a tool that is used to make work easier for people. A bicycle, scissors, a hammer, and a lawnmower are all examples of machines. Ask students if they can imagine building a house without a hammer and nails. Ask them to think about how difficult it would be to cut a shape out of paper without scissors. If people have to do a very big job, such as building a big house, a big machine is needed.

2 Introduce the Vocabulary

Content Vocabulary Point to each pictured word. Read the word aloud and have students echo you. Then have them write the word on the line. Explain phonetic structures that are unfamiliar to your students. Guide students to find the vocabulary words that are names of big machines (*backhoe, bulldozer, concrete mixing truck, crane, dump truck, loader*). Discuss word meanings as needed.

Words to Know Point to each word and read it aloud. Have students echo you. Point out the following:

- The word *drum* is a multiple-meaning word. In this text, *drum* means "a barrel-shaped metal container."
- The *ch* in *chute* has a /**sh**/ sound.

CCSS: RIT 2.1, 2.2, 2.3, 2.4, 2.6, 2.7   W 2.2, 2.8   SL 2.2

3 Read the Texts

Student Text Guide students in reading the text together aloud. Then have them retell the main idea and give details about big machines they learned from the text.

Teacher's Complex Text Have students look at the pictures in their text and listen as you read aloud the Teacher's Complex Text on page 24. Say: *Look at the pictures and listen as I read more information about big machines.*

4 Reading Comprehension Activities

Guide students through completing the activities on pages 27 and 28. Encourage them to look at their text to find information.

5 Close Reading Activity

Oral Discussion Use the Oral Discussion Questions on the right to guide students in a discussion about what they have read and heard. Before you begin, make sure each student has colored pencils and his or her text.

Begin by reading aloud a question. Then have students answer the question and mark the answer in their text.

6 Vocabulary Activity

Review the vocabulary on the *Dictionary* page. Then guide students through the *Words I Know* activity.

7 Writing Activities

Guide students through the first writing activity, *I Can Write*. Then have them read aloud their sentences to a partner. Discuss the writing prompt on the second writing page, *What I Learned*. As an informal assessment of students' understanding, have them write and illustrate their paragraphs independently.

Oral Discussion Questions

1. How many types of big machines are described in the text? (*six*) Draw a red line under each heading that names a big machine. (*backhoe, bulldozer, concrete mixing truck, crane, dump truck, loader*)

2. Which big machine crawls on its own tracks and has a big blade on its front? (*bulldozer*) Make an orange X by the paragraph. What does the blade do? (*The blade can push soil, trees, and things as big as a car.*) Draw a green line under the sentence that tells you.

3. Why would you use a loader to remove snow? (*A loader has a bucket on the front to scoop up snow, move it, and load it into a dump truck.*) Circle in black the number of the paragraph that tells you this. (*paragraph 6*)

4. Name two jobs a concrete mixing truck can do. (*1. It mixes concrete. 2. It carries concrete to the job.*) Make a blue X next to the paragraph that tells you. (*paragraph 3*) What is the chute for? (*The chute moves concrete out of the truck.*)

5. How do you think the backhoe got its name? Clue: Think about the direction in which it digs. (*It digs backward instead of forward.*) Draw a yellow line under a word that gave you a clue. Look at the picture of the backhoe. Point to the part that digs backward.

Science
Teacher's Complex Text

Big Machines

We see big machines at work all around us.
There are big machines for all kinds of jobs.

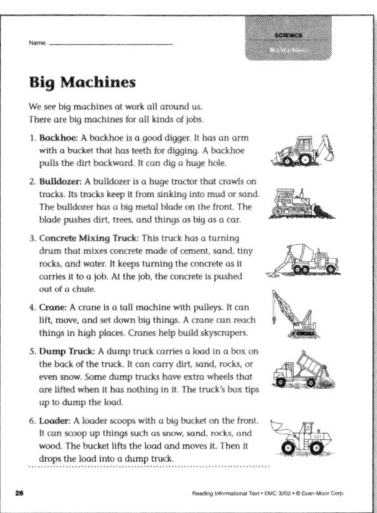
student text, pg. 26

1. **Backhoe:** A backhoe is a powerful digger. It has an arm made of two main parts. The arm of the backhoe bends just like your arm bends at your elbow. The backhoe's arm can also swing to the left and right. At the end of the arm is a bucket with teeth for digging. When a backhoe digs, it pulls the dirt backward. A backhoe can dig a huge hole or remove a rock or a giant tree stump.

2. **Bulldozer:** A bulldozer is a heavy tractor that crawls along on tracks that keep it from sinking into mud or sand. It has a huge blade on its front that can push soil, trees, broken concrete, and objects as big as a car. The back of the bulldozer has a ripper that works like a claw for breaking up hard earth. A bulldozer is used for many kinds of jobs needed in the military, in mining, on farms, and other places.

3. **Concrete Mixing Truck:** A concrete mixing truck has a turning drum that holds concrete. Concrete is made from cement, sand, gravel, and water. The truck mixes the concrete while carrying it to a job. The drum has a scraper inside that mixes the concrete to keep it from getting hard. At a worksite, the liquid concrete pours out of the drum and down a chute. The chute directs the concrete to where it is needed.

4. **Crane:** A crane is a tall machine with pulleys. It can lift, move, and set down heavy materials. A crane is used for building skyscrapers, because it can lift and move building materials in high places. It is also used in shipyards and factories.

5. **Dump Truck:** A dump truck carries materials such as dirt, gravel, and snow. Some dump trucks have extra wheels on each side that can be raised or lowered. When it has a heavy load, the extra wheels are lowered. When a load needs to be dumped, the box on the back of a dump truck tips up and the gate on the box opens.

6. **Loader:** A loader has a large, square bucket on the front. It can scoop up things such as sand, gravel, rocks, and wood pieces. The bucket lifts and moves the load. Then it drops the load into a dump truck. A loader can clear a construction site, remove snow, and do many jobs on a farm.

Name: _____

SCIENCE

Big Machines

Dictionary

Look at the picture. Read the word.
Write the word on the line.

Content Vocabulary

backhoe

_____

bulldozer

_____

concrete mixing truck

_____

crane

_____

dump truck

_____

loader

_____

Words to Know

bucket	cement	chute
drum	metal	pulley
scoop	skyscrapers	wheels

© Evan-Moor Corp. • EMC 3202 • Reading Informational Text

Name: _____

SCIENCE

Big Machines

Big Machines

We see big machines at work all around us.
There are big machines for all kinds of jobs.

1. **Backhoe:** A backhoe is a good digger. It has an arm with a bucket that has teeth for digging. A backhoe pulls the dirt backward. It can dig a huge hole.

2. **Bulldozer:** A bulldozer is a huge tractor that crawls on tracks. Its tracks keep it from sinking into mud or sand. The bulldozer has a big metal blade on the front. The blade pushes dirt, trees, and things as big as a car.

3. **Concrete Mixing Truck:** This truck has a turning drum that mixes concrete made of cement, sand, tiny rocks, and water. It keeps turning the concrete as it carries it to a job. At the job, the concrete is pushed out of a chute.

4. **Crane:** A crane is a tall machine with pulleys. It can lift, move, and set down big things. A crane can reach things in high places. Cranes help build skyscrapers.

5. **Dump Truck:** A dump truck carries a load in a box on the back of the truck. It can carry dirt, sand, rocks, or even snow. Some dump trucks have extra wheels that are lifted when it has nothing in it. The truck's box tips up to dump the load.

6. **Loader:** A loader scoops with a big bucket on the front. It can scoop up things such as snow, sand, rocks, and wood. The bucket lifts the load and moves it. Then it drops the load into a dump truck.

Name: _____

SCIENCE

Big Machines

I Read and Understand

Read and answer.

1. A drum and a chute are parts on a _____.
   - ○ dump truck
   - ○ loader
   - ○ concrete mixing truck

2. A _____ has tracks and a blade.
   - ○ scoop
   - ○ bulldozer
   - ○ backhoe

3. The pulleys on a _____ help it lift things.
   - ○ loader
   - ○ crane
   - ○ backhoe

4. A _____ has a big bucket on the front.
   - ○ backhoe
   - ○ dump truck
   - ○ loader

5. A loader loads dirt into a _____.
   - ○ dump truck
   - ○ concrete mixing truck
   - ○ bulldozer

© Evan-Moor Corp. • EMC 3202 • Reading Informational Text

Name: _____

SCIENCE

Big Machines

I Read Closely

Read the text closely.
Finish the sentence with the words used in the text.

concrete mixing truck

1. The truck mixes concrete as it
_____
_____

backhoe

2. When a backhoe digs, it pulls
_____
_____

loader

3. The bucket lifts
_____
_____

bulldozer

4. A bulldozer is a huge tractor that
_____
_____

28   Reading Informational Text • EMC 3202 • © Evan-Moor Corp.

Name: _____

SCIENCE

Big Machines

Words I Know

Read and answer.

1. My bike has two ____.
   - ○ skyscrapers
   - ○ buckets
   - ○ wheels

2. Dad dug a hole with a ____.
   - ○ backhoe
   - ○ drum
   - ○ chute

3. A ____ brought sand for our sandbox.
   - ○ concrete mixing truck
   - ○ dump truck
   - ○ backhoe

4. The ____ lifted a load of bricks.
   - ○ cement
   - ○ crane
   - ○ chute

5. Concrete is mixed in a turning ____.
   - ○ drum
   - ○ scoop
   - ○ wheel

6. Those big trees were moved by a ____.
   - ○ pulley
   - ○ bulldozer
   - ○ metal

Name: _____

SCIENCE

Big Machines

I Can Write

Look at the picture.
Write about the work the machine can do.

backhoe

_____
_____
_____
_____

dump truck

_____
_____
_____
_____

loader

_____
_____
_____
_____

Name: _____

SCIENCE

Big Machines

What I Learned

Write about a big machine. Describe what it is and tell about the work it can do. Then draw a picture of the machine at work.

_____

_____

_____

_____

_____

_____

© Evan-Moor Corp. • EMC 3202 • Reading Informational Text

LEVEL K

Geography
Big Island Map

Lesson Objective Students will learn about some physical features of the island of Hawaii on a grid map.

Content Knowledge Maps show geographical features and can be used to locate specific places.

Lesson Preparation

Reproduce and distribute to each student one copy of the dictionary page (p. 35), the student text (p. 36), and the activity pages (pp. 37–41).

Learn

1. Build Background

2. Introduce the Vocabulary
   Dictionary

3. Read the Texts
   Big Island Map
   Teacher's Complex Text

Analyze

4. Reading Comprehension Activities
   I Read and Understand
   I Read Closely

5. Close Reading Activity
   Oral Discussion Questions

6. Vocabulary Activity
   Words I Know

Write

7. Writing Activities
   I Can Write
   What I Learned

1 Build Background

Explain that a landform, such as a hill or valley, is a part of Earth's surface. An island is another type of landform. An island is land surrounded on all sides by water. Some islands, such as the islands of Hawaii, are created when volcanoes erupt. Hot melted rock called lava erupts from a volcano. The lava comes from deep inside Earth. The lava builds up and cools, forming new and bigger islands.

2 Introduce the Vocabulary

Content Vocabulary Point to each pictured word. Read the word aloud and have students echo you. Then have them write the word on the line. Explain phonetic structures that are unfamiliar to your students. Tell students that in the word *island*, the *s* is silent. Discuss word meanings as needed.

Words to Know Point to each word and read it aloud. Have students echo you. Point out the following:

- The word *sleeping* is a multiple-meaning word. In this text, *sleeping* means "quiet" or "not erupting."
- A *ranch* is a large farm for cattle, sheep, or horses.
- A *volcano* is a mountain with a hole at the top that lets hot lava out.

CCSS: RIT 2.1, 2.2, 2.3, 2.4, 2.6, 2.7   W 2.2, 2.8   SL 2.2

3 Read the Texts

Student Text Guide students in reading the text together aloud. Help them read aloud the pronunciation guides. Then have them retell the main idea and give details they learned about the Big Island from the text.

Teacher's Complex Text Have students look at the map in their text and listen as you read aloud the Teacher's Complex Text on page 34. Say: *Look at the map as I read more information about the Big Island of Hawaii.*

4 Reading Comprehension Activities

Guide students through completing the activities on pages 37 and 38. Encourage them to look at their text to find information.

5 Close Reading Activity

Oral Discussion Use the Oral Discussion Questions on the right to guide students in a discussion about what they have read and heard. Before you begin, make sure each student has colored pencils and his or her text.

Begin by reading aloud a question. Then have students answer the question and mark the answer in their text.

6 Vocabulary Activity

Review the vocabulary on the *Dictionary* page. Then guide students through the *Words I Know* activity.

7 Writing Activities

Guide students through the first writing activity, *I Can Write*. Then have them compare their charts with a partner. Discuss the writing prompt on the second writing page, *What I Learned*. As an informal assessment of students' understanding, have them write their paragraphs independently.

Oral Discussion Questions

1. Name two places that are both named Hawaii. (*the state of Hawaii and the island of Hawaii*) What is the nickname that helps tell them apart? (*The Big Island is another name for the island of Hawaii.*) Draw a blue line under the nickname.

2. Which volcano on the Big Island is active? (*Kilauea*) Circle its name with red. What do you think is the difference between an active volcano and a sleeping volcano? (*Red-hot lava flows from an active volcano; so a sleeping volcano probably doesn't have hot lava flowing from it.*)

3. How does Kilauea help the Big Island grow bigger all the time? (*Red-hot lava flows from Kilauea all the time. The lava cools into rock and builds up the island.*) Draw a purple line under the sentences that tell you.

4. Where could you go on the Big Island to learn about coffee plants? (*You could go to Kona Coffee Farm.*) Find it on the map and make a brown X on it. (*F2*)

5. Where could you go to see an active volcano? (*Kilauea*) Find it on the map and make a red X on it. (*E5*)

6. Explain how to find what is located at B1 on the map. (*Answers will vary.*) What is its name? (*Hapuna Beach*) What could you do there? (*You could swim, dive, and enjoy the sun.*)

Geography
Teacher's Complex Text

Big Island Map

Can you name the largest island in the United States? The state of Hawaii is made up of a chain of 132 islands that were created from volcanoes. The islands stretch for more than a thousand miles in the Pacific Ocean. Many of them are tiny, and no one lives there. However, there are eight main islands where people live, and the largest is called Hawaii. It's easy to confuse the name of the island with the state, so the island of Hawaii has another name. It is known as the Big Island. The name fits for more than one reason. One reason is that it is the biggest island in the state of Hawaii. Another reason is that it is also the biggest island in the United States. A third reason is that because of an active volcano, the Big Island is growing bigger all the time!

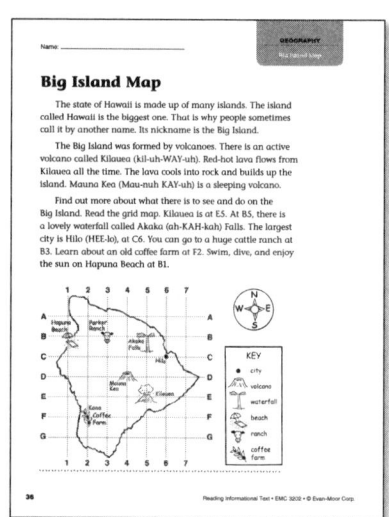

student text, pg. 36

The Big Island of Hawaii was formed by five volcanoes. One volcano called Kilauea (kil-uh-WAY-uh) is an active volcano. It has been erupting steadily since 1983. Red-hot lava flows from Kilauea all the time. Some of it spills into the ocean, sending up clouds of steam. The lava cools into rock and builds up the island. Another volcano, Mauna Kea, is the tallest mountain on Earth. Scientists have measured it from its base deep in the ocean to its very top, thousands of feet above sea level. This mountain is a sleeping volcano. A sleeping volcano is one that hasn't exploded hot lava, or erupted, in a long time. A sleeping volcano might still erupt someday.

Read the grid map to find some great places to visit on the Big Island of Hawaii. The numbers going across the top and bottom, and the letters going down the sides of the map name squares on the grid. The compass rose shows the directions: north, south, east, west. For example, let's find Hilo (HEE-lo), the largest city on the Big Island. To find Hilo at C6, move your finger across the map at row C until you find where it meets column 6. That square is C6. At E5, you can see the volcano Kilauea erupting. At B5, there is a lovely waterfall at Akaka (ah-KAH-kah) Falls State Park. You can visit a huge cattle ranch, called Parker Ranch, at B3. Learn how coffee is grown at the Kona Coffee Living History Farm at F2. Swim, dive, and enjoy the sun on Hapuna Beach at B1.

Name: _____

GEOGRAPHY

Big Island Map

Dictionary

Look at the picture. Read the word.
Write the word on the line.

Content Vocabulary

active volcano

_____

cattle

_____

coffee

_____

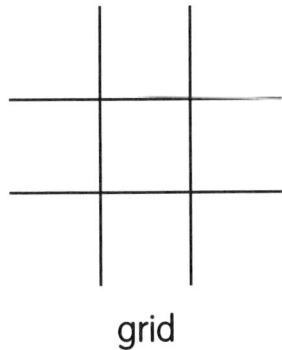

grid

_____

island

_____

waterfall

_____

Words to Know

beach	flows	Hawaii
lava	lovely	nickname
ranch	sleeping	volcano

© Evan-Moor Corp. • EMC 3202 • Reading Informational Text

Name: _____

GEOGRAPHY

Big Island Map

Big Island Map

The state of Hawaii is made up of many islands. The island called Hawaii is the biggest one. That is why people sometimes call it by another name. Its nickname is the Big Island.

The Big Island was formed by volcanoes. There is an active volcano called Kilauea (kil-uh-WAY-uh). Red-hot lava flows from Kilauea all the time. The lava cools into rock and builds up the island. Mauna Kea (Mau-nuh KAY-uh) is a sleeping volcano.

Find out more about what there is to see and do on the Big Island. Read the grid map. Kilauea is at E5. At B5, there is a lovely waterfall called Akaka (ah-KAH-kah) Falls. The largest city is Hilo (HEE-lo), at C6. You can go to a huge cattle ranch at B3. Learn about an old coffee farm at F2. Swim, dive, and enjoy the sun on Hapuna Beach at B1.

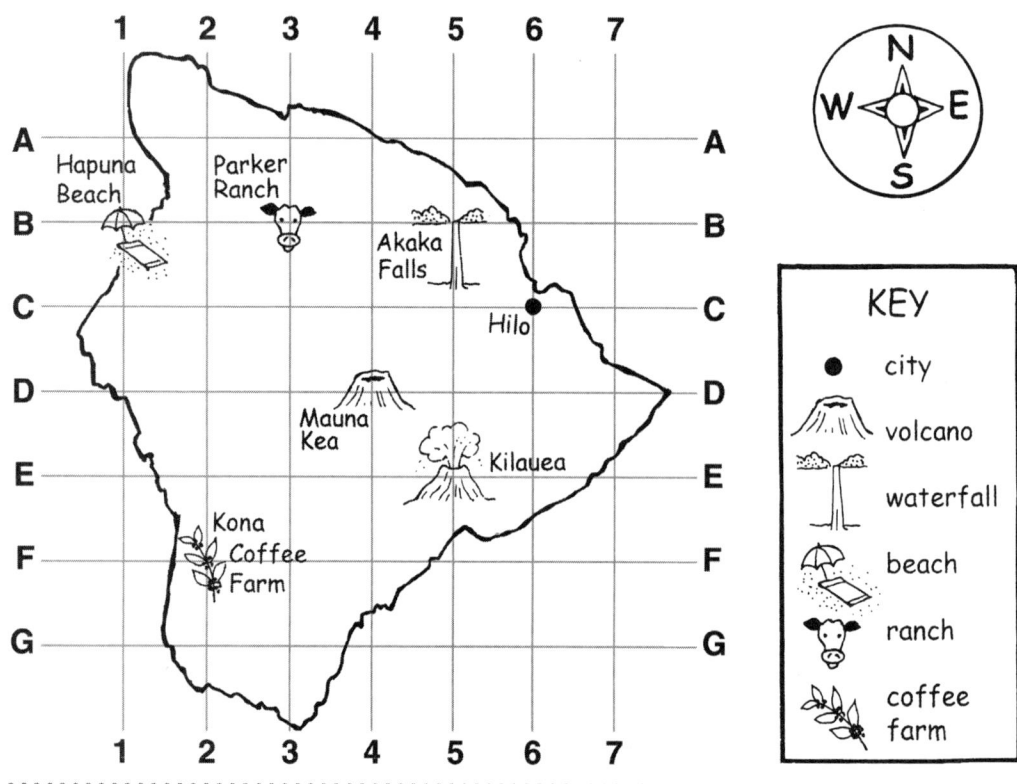

Name: _____

GEOGRAPHY

Big Island Map

I Read and Understand

Read and answer.

1. Hawaii is the name of _____.
   - ○ a volcano
   - ○ a state and an island
   - ○ a cattle ranch

2. The Big Island was formed by _____.
   - ○ volcanoes
   - ○ coffee farms
   - ○ waterfalls

3. Where is Hilo on the map grid?
   - ○ B6
   - ○ C6
   - ○ D5

4. What can you find at B3 on the map?
   - ○ a coffee farm
   - ○ a cattle ranch
   - ○ a waterfall

5. Where can you find an active volcano on the map?
   - ○ E5
   - ○ B5
   - ○ D4

© Evan-Moor Corp. • EMC 3202 • Reading Informational Text

Name: _____

GEOGRAPHY

Big Island Map

I Read Closely

Read the text closely.
Finish the sentence with the words used in the text.

Kilauea

1. Red-hot lava _____
_____

Big Island

2. Its nickname _____
_____

waterfall

3. At B5, there is a _____
_____

beach

4. Swim, dive, and enjoy the sun
_____
_____

Name: _____

GEOGRAPHY

Big Island Map

Words I Know

Read and answer.

1. Cows live on a _____ ranch.
   - ○ coffee
   - ○ dive
   - ○ cattle

2. Let's go swimming today at the _____.
   - ○ volcano
   - ○ beach
   - ○ lava

3. Lava flows from _____ volcano.
   - ○ an active
   - ○ a sleeping
   - ○ a cool

4. You can use a _____ map to find places in Hawaii.
   - ○ nickname
   - ○ ranch
   - ○ grid

5. _____ has water all around it.
   - ○ An island
   - ○ A ranch
   - ○ A nickname

6. The _____ spills over a cliff.
   - ○ city
   - ○ waterfall
   - ○ ranch

© Evan-Moor Corp. • EMC 3202 • Reading Informational Text

Name: _____

I Can Write

GEOGRAPHY

Big Island Map

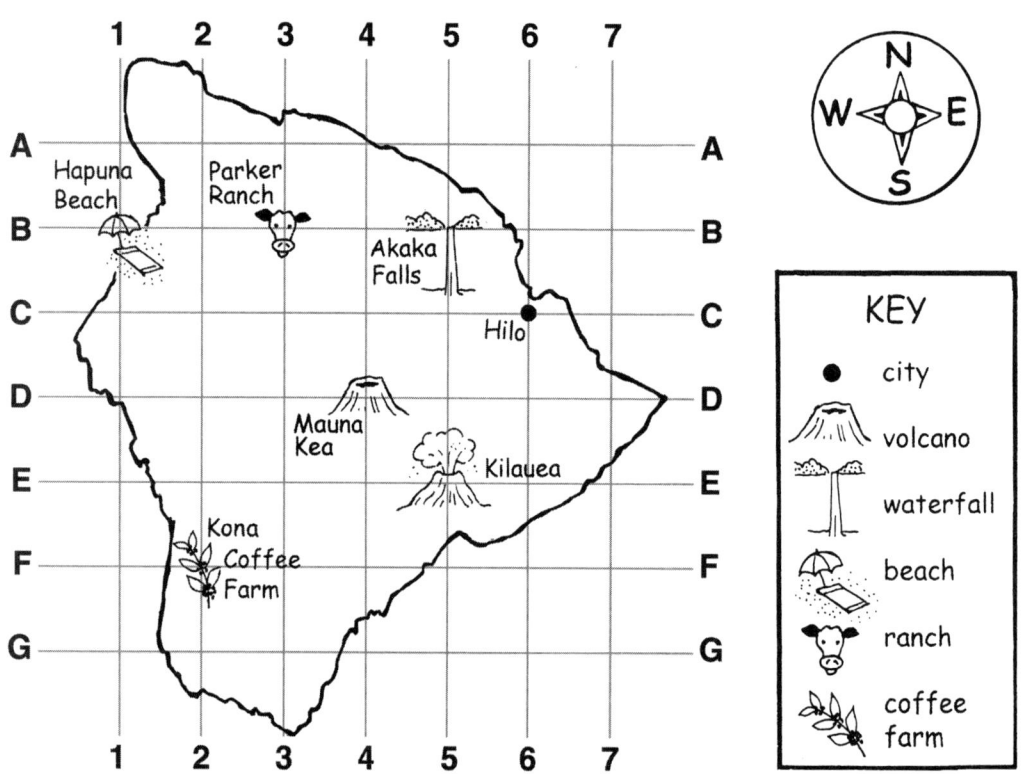

Look at the grid map of Hawaii.
Then fill in the chart about places on the map.
Each row is missing something. The first row is done for you.

Place Name	What Is It?	Where Is It?
Parker Ranch	ranch	B3
Kilauea		E5
Kona Coffee Farm	coffee farm	
Hapuna Beach	beach	
	waterfall	B5
Hilo	city	
	volcano	D4

40 Reading Informational Text • EMC 3202 • © Evan-Moor Corp.

Name: _____

GEOGRAPHY

Big Island Map

What I Learned

Write a paragraph that tells about three places to visit on the Big Island. Include grid letters and numbers. Use facts from your *I Can Write* chart.

Social Studies
TOMS Shoes

Lesson Objective Students will learn about a company, TOMS Shoes, and how it helps children.

Content Knowledge Human wants and needs, scarcity, and consumer choice are basic economic concepts.

Lesson Preparation

Reproduce and distribute to each student one copy of the dictionary page (p. 45), the student text (p. 46), and the activity pages (pp. 47–51).

Learn

1 Build Background

2 Introduce the Vocabulary
Dictionary

3 Read the Texts
TOMS Shoes
Teacher's Complex Text

Analyze

4 Reading Comprehension Activities
I Read and Understand
I Read Closely

5 Close Reading Activity
Oral Discussion Questions

6 Vocabulary Activity
Words I Know

Write

7 Writing Activities
I Can Write
What I Learned

1 Build Background

Explain to students that people wear shoes to protect their feet. Tell students that a person's foot has 26 bones. Feet have an amazing design. They carry a person's body weight, and take a pounding when they walk or run. Shoes protect feet from freezing snow and ice, from hot sands and pavement, from sharp stones, and from insect bites. People have been wearing shoes for thousands of years.

2 Introduce the Vocabulary

Content Vocabulary Point to each pictured word. Read the word aloud and have students echo you. Then have them write the word on the line. Explain phonetic structures that are unfamiliar to your students. Point out the following:

- The word *sickness* ends with *-ness*. *Sickness* means "an illness or disease."

- *Argentina* is a country in South America. Show students Argentina on a map.

Words to Know Point to each word and read it aloud. Have students echo you. Point out that *company* is a multiple-meaning word. Explain that in this text, *company* means "a business."

CCSS: **RIT** 2.1, 2.2, 2.3, 2.4, 2.6   **W** 2.2, 2.8   **SL** 2.2

3 Read the Texts

Student Text Guide students in reading the text together aloud. Point out that the text tells about *Blake Mycoskie*, who started a shoe company. Then have them retell the main idea and give details they learned about TOMS Shoes from the text.

Teacher's Complex Text Have students look at the picture in their text and listen as you read the Teacher's Complex Text on page 44. Say: *Look at the picture and listen as I read you more information about TOMS Shoes.*

4 Reading Comprehension Activities

Guide students through completing the activities on pages 47 and 48. Encourage them to look at their text to find information.

5 Close Reading Activity

Oral Discussion Use the Oral Discussion Questions on the right to guide students in a discussion about what they have read and heard. Before you begin, make sure each student has colored pencils and his or her text.

Begin by reading aloud a question. Then have students answer the question and mark the answer in their text.

6 Vocabulary Activity

Review the vocabulary on the *Dictionary* page. Then guide students through the *Words I Know* activity.

7 Writing Activities

Guide students through the *I Can Write* activity. Then have them read aloud their sentences to a partner. Discuss the writing prompt in the *What I Learned* activity. As an informal assessment of students' understanding, have them write and illustrate their paragraphs independently.

Oral Discussion Questions

1. Most people who start a shoe company only want to sell shoes. Why did Blake Mycoskie start his shoe company? (*He wanted to give shoes to children who needed them.*) Draw a purple line under the sentence that tells the answer.

2. Name two ways in which Argentina was important in the story of TOMS Shoes. (*1. When Blake Mycoskie visited Argentina in 2006, he saw many children without shoes. 2. He also saw farmers wearing a simple type of shoe.*) Draw a green line under two sentences that tell the answers.

3. Name two ways in which shoes help children. (*1. Shoes help children to get to school. 2. Shoes also help children to stay healthy.*) Draw a red line under two sentences that tell the answer.

4. By 2013, how many pairs of shoes did TOMS Shoes give away? (*By 2013, TOMS Shoes had given away more than two million pairs of shoes to children in over 50 countries.*) Draw an orange line under the sentence that tells the answer.

5. The words "one for one" appear in the text. Circle the words in yellow. What does "one for one" mean? (*Paragraph 1; It means sell one pair, and one free pair is given to a child in need.*)

6. Blake Mycoskie believes that people can make the world a better place. How? (*He says people can give to others and make tomorrow, or the future, better.*)

Social Studies
Teacher's Complex Text

TOMS Shoes

Blake Mycoskie wanted to give shoes to children who needed them. So he started a shoe company. TOMS Shoes is a company that works in a different way than most companies do. TOMS Shoes was founded for a special purpose. It was to give to those in need. When TOMS® sells a pair of shoes, one free pair is given to a child in need. Blake Mycoskie calls this idea "One for One®." It is a way for people who <u>want</u> new shoes to give to children who <u>need</u> new shoes.

Blake Mycoskie loves to read and travel. Before he started TOMS Shoes, he was on a TV show with his sister. It was called *The Amazing Race*. They raced to places around the world. They came very close to winning a million-dollar prize. When Mycoskie visited Argentina in 2006, he saw many children without shoes. He also saw a simple type of shoe, called an alpargata (all-par-GAH-tuh). It was made of cloth and it slipped on. Farmers in Argentina had worn this type of shoe for hundreds of years. That is how Mycoskie got the idea for his simple shoe.

student text, pg. 46

Why are shoes important for children? Shoes help children to get schooling. Many children must walk to school without shoes. Some children don't go to school because they don't have shoes. Shoes also help children to stay healthy. Many children play outdoors. They have nothing to keep their bare feet from being hurt. In some places, children get sick from not wearing shoes. They pick up a sickness from the soil they walk on. The sickness makes it difficult for them to walk.

The new TOMS Shoes company grew quickly, because people wanted to buy the shoes, and they wanted to help. In 2006, TOMS Shoes gave away ten thousand pairs of new shoes. By 2013, TOMS Shoes had given away more than two million pairs. Children in over 50 countries received new shoes for free. One more thing you might be wondering about—why is Mycoskie's company called "TOMS?" TOMS comes from the word *tomorrow*. He first named his company "Shoes for a Better Tomorrow." The name was shortened to "Tomorrow's Shoes." Then it became "TOMS." Blake Mycoskie tells people to think about giving to others in everything they do. He believes this is the way to make *tomorrow* better.

Name: _____

SOCIAL STUDIES

TOMS Shoes

Dictionary

Look at the picture. Read the word.
Write the word on the line.

Content Vocabulary

Argentina

_____

million

_____

pair

_____

shoes

_____

sickness

_____

soil

_____

Words to Know

cloth	company	different
everything	healthy	hurt
idea	simple	tomorrow

TOMS Shoes

Blake Mycoskie wanted to give shoes to children who needed them. To do this, he started a shoe company called TOMS Shoes. TOMS Shoes is different from most companies. When TOMS sells a pair of shoes, one free pair is given to a child who does not have shoes. Blake Mycoskie calls this idea "One for One."

In 2006, Blake Mycoskie visited Argentina. He saw many children without shoes. He also saw a simple shoe that was made of cloth. The shoe was made of strong cloth like the kind used to make pants. Farmers in Argentina had worn this kind of shoe for hundreds of years. That is how Mycoskie got the idea for his shoes.

Why do children need shoes? Shoes help children to stay healthy. Many children play outside and do not have shoes to keep their feet from being hurt. In some places, children get sick from not wearing shoes. They pick up a sickness from the soil they walk on. Some children don't go to school because they don't have shoes.

In 2006, TOMS Shoes gave away ten thousand pairs of new shoes. By 2013, TOMS had given away more than two million pairs to children in more than 50 countries. Blake Mycoskie tells people to find a way to give to others in everything they do. He believes giving to others can make tomorrow better.

Name: _____

SOCIAL STUDIES
TOMS Shoes

I Read and Understand

Read and answer.

1. TOMS Shoes is _____.
   - ○ a different kind of cloth
   - ○ a new school
   - ○ a shoe company

2. Children in Argentina needed _____.
   - ○ sickness
   - ○ shoes
   - ○ ideas

3. TOMS sells shoes and gives _____ away.
   - ○ shoes
   - ○ socks
   - ○ books

4. Children didn't go to school because _____.
   - ○ it was too far
   - ○ there was no school
   - ○ they needed shoes

5. Farmers wore _____ shoes.
   - ○ simple
   - ○ kind
   - ○ brown

Name: _____

I Read Closely

SOCIAL STUDIES
TOMS Shoes

Read the text closely.
Finish the sentence with the words used in the text.

1. When Blake Mycoskie visited Argentina in 2006, he

   _____

   _____

2. When TOMS sells a pair of shoes, one free pair

   _____

   _____

3. By 2013, TOMS had given away shoes to

   _____

   _____

4. Farmers in Argentina had worn this kind of

   _____

   _____

Name: _____

SOCIAL STUDIES

TOMS Shoes

Words I Know

Read and answer.

1. My pants are made of _____.
   - ○ ideas
   - ○ soil
   - ○ cloth

2. The bad _____ went away after two days.
   - ○ healthy
   - ○ sickness
   - ○ simple

3. I can find _____ on a map.
   - ○ Argentina
   - ○ tomorrow
   - ○ sickness

4. We need _____ to walk to school.
   - ○ shoes
   - ○ soil
   - ○ tomorrow

5. The day after today is _____.
   - ○ company
   - ○ tomorrow
   - ○ everything

6. A _____ of shoes means there are two.
   - ○ simple
   - ○ pair
   - ○ different

© Evan-Moor Corp. • EMC 3202 • Reading Informational Text

Name: _____

SOCIAL STUDIES

TOMS Shoes

I Can Write

Look at the pictures.
Write something about TOMS Shoes for each one.

new shoes

_____
_____
_____

school

_____
_____
_____

soil

_____
_____
_____

Name: _____

SOCIAL STUDIES

TOMS Shoes

What I Learned

Write about TOMS Shoes.
Tell how this shoe company helps children.

_____

_____

_____

_____

_____

Draw a picture about what you wrote.

LEVEL L

Social Studies
Rosa Parks Rides the Bus

Lesson Objective Students will learn about Rosa Parks wanting to be treated fairly. Students will understand how her experience started a movement that helped improve equality.

Content Knowledge People in history have contributed to society and made a difference in improving equality.

Lesson Preparation

Reproduce and distribute to each student one copy of the dictionary page (p. 55), the student text (p. 56), and the activity pages (pp. 57–61).

Learn

1. Build Background

2. Introduce the Vocabulary
   Dictionary

3. Read the Texts
   Rosa Parks Rides the Bus
   Teacher's Complex Text

Analyze

4. Reading Comprehension Activities
   I Read and Understand
   I Read Closely

5. Close Reading Activity
   Oral Discussion Questions

6. Vocabulary Activity
   Words I Know

Write

7. Writing Activities
   I Can Write
   What I Learned

1 Build Background

Explain to students that *equal rights* means that everyone will be treated fairly no matter what they look like, what they believe, or what they can do. Dr. Martin Luther King, Jr. was the main leader of the movement to gain equal rights for African Americans in the 1950s and 1960s. Because of Dr. King and other leaders, many laws were changed. They helped improve equality for all.

2 Introduce the Vocabulary

Content Vocabulary Point to each pictured word. Read the word aloud and have students echo you. Then have them write the word on the line. Explain phonetic structures that are unfamiliar to students. Discuss word meanings as needed. Point out the following:

- The word *fine* is a multiple-meaning word. Explain that in this text, *fine* means "money paid as punishment for breaking a law."

Words to Know Point to each word and read it aloud. Have students echo you. Point out the following:

- Montgomery is a city in the state of Alabama. Guide students in locating it on a map.

- In this text, a *right* is something that the law allows you to do.

CCSS: **RIT** 2.1, 2.2, 2.3, 2.4, 2.6, 2.7   **W** 2.2, 2.8   **SL** 2.2

3 Read the Texts

Student Text Guide students in reading the text together aloud. Then have them retell the main idea and give details they learned about Rosa Parks from the text.

Teacher's Complex Text Have students look at the picture in their text and listen as you read aloud the Teacher's Complex Text on page 54. Say: *Look at the picture and listen as I read more information about Rosa Parks.*

4 Reading Comprehension Activities

Guide students through completing the activities on pages 57 and 58. Encourage them to look at their text to find information.

5 Close Reading Activity

Oral Discussion Use the Oral Discussion Questions on the right to guide students in a discussion about what they have read and heard. Before you begin, make sure each student has colored pencils and his or her text.

Begin by reading aloud a question. Then have students answer the question and mark the answer in their text.

6 Vocabulary Activity

Review the vocabulary on the *Dictionary* page. Then guide students through the *Words I Know* activity.

7 Writing Activities

Guide students through the first writing activity, *I Can Write*. Then have them read aloud their sentences to a partner. Discuss the writing prompt on the second writing page, *What I Learned*. As an informal assessment of students' understanding of the topic, have them write and illustrate their paragraphs independently.

Oral Discussion Questions

1. In which paragraph do we find out what kind of work Rosa Parks did? (*paragraph 1*) Draw a purple line under the sentence that tells you. (*Mrs. Rosa Parks finished her long day at work as a seamstress.*)

2. What did the Jim Crow laws say that African Americans had to do? (*Jim Crow laws said African Americans had to sit in the back of the bus, and give up their seats if a white person didn't have one.*) What did Rosa Parks know she had a right to do? (*She had a right to sit in a seat and to sit where she wanted.*) Make a blue X next to the paragraph that tells about this.

3. What did Rosa Parks say when she was told to give up her seat? (*She said no.*) The author uses two words to describe how Rosa Parks said no. Find each sentence and circle in orange the words the author chose. (*quietly, bravely*)

4. How did African American people in Montgomery show they thought the laws were unfair? (*People stopped riding the buses.*) Draw a yellow line under the sentence that tells you.

5. Who finally stopped the unfair laws? (*The judges stopped the laws.*) Draw a green line under the sentence that tells about it.

6. A biography tells about a person's life. Is a biography fiction or nonfiction? (*nonfiction*) Was Rosa Parks a real person? (*yes*)

© Evan-Moor Corp. • EMC 3202 • Reading Informational Text

Social Studies
Teacher's Complex Text

Rosa Parks Rides the Bus

It was December 1, 1955, in Montgomery, Alabama. In those days, it was as if people who were African American and people who were white lived in different worlds. Laws of segregation, called "Jim Crow" laws, kept them apart. Mrs. Rosa Parks worked as a seamstress in a department store. She finished her long day at work. She put on her hat and coat to go home. Mrs. Parks waited at the bus stop. When the bus came, Rosa Parks got on the bus and sat down.

The Jim Crow laws said many things about what African American people had to do. The laws said that African American people must sit only in the back of the bus. The Jim Crow laws also said that if there weren't enough seats, then African American people had to give up their seats to white people. Rosa Parks was African American. The bus made more stops and filled up with people. The bus driver told Mrs. Parks to stand up and give her seat to a white man. Rosa Parks quietly said, "No." Rosa Parks knew she would go to jail, but she wanted to be treated fairly. It was her right to sit where she wanted. The bus driver called the police. Mrs. Parks was taken to jail. She had broken the Jim Crow law, so she had to pay a fine of ten dollars.

Soon, other African Americans heard about how Rosa Parks had bravely said no. They organized a bus boycott to protest the law. Their leader was a young minister named Martin Luther King, Jr. Thousands of people joined together and stopped riding the city buses. Instead, they walked to work and school. They rode in carpools together. They rode in taxis. At the same time, people worked to have the laws changed. At last, the judges of the Supreme Court of the United States said that the Jim Crow laws were unfair and must be stopped, because they went against the Constitution of the United States. The Jim Crow laws were no more. African Americans were to have the same rights as white Americans. After 381 days, the bus boycott ended. Rosa Parks had done a very important thing when she said no. Today, she is remembered as the mother of the civil rights movement for equality.

student text, pg. 56

Name: _____

SOCIAL STUDIES

Rosa Parks Rides the Bus

Dictionary

Look at the picture. Read the word.
Write the word on the line.

Content Vocabulary

fine

_____

jail

_____

judges

_____

police

_____

Rosa Parks

_____

seamstress

_____

Words to Know

African American	Alabama	bravely	bus stop
December	important	Montgomery	quietly
rights	taxi	treated	unfair

© Evan-Moor Corp. • EMC 3202 • Reading Informational Text

55

Rosa Parks Rides the Bus

The day was December 1, 1955, in Montgomery, Alabama. Mrs. Rosa Parks finished her long day at work as a seamstress. She put on her hat and coat to go home. Mrs. Parks waited at the bus stop. When the bus came, she got on and sat down.

At that time, there were laws called Jim Crow laws. The laws said African American people must sit in the back of the bus. They also said that if the bus was full, then African Americans had to let white people have their seats. Rosa Parks was African American. Mrs. Parks sat in a seat behind the white people. The bus made more stops and filled up with people. The bus driver told Mrs. Parks to stand up and give her seat to a white man. Rosa Parks wanted to be treated fairly. She quietly said, "No." The police came and took Mrs. Parks to jail. Because she had broken a Jim Crow law, she had to pay a fine.

Soon, African American people heard about how Rosa Parks had bravely said no. They stopped riding the city buses. They walked or rode in cars and taxis to work and school. They didn't ride the buses for 381 days. During this time, African American people worked to have the laws changed. At last, the judges said that the Jim Crow laws were unfair and must be stopped. African Americans now had the same rights as white Americans. Rosa Parks did something important when she said no.

Name: _____

SOCIAL STUDIES

Rosa Parks Rides the Bus

I Read and Understand

Read and answer.

1. After work, Rosa Parks _____.
    - ○ took a taxi
    - ○ walked home
    - ○ rode the bus

2. White people _____.
    - ○ sat in the back
    - ○ sat in the front
    - ○ did not ride the bus

3. Rosa Parks would not _____.
    - ○ pay a fine
    - ○ give up her seat
    - ○ sit down quietly

4. African American people stopped _____.
    - ○ going to work
    - ○ going to school
    - ○ riding the bus

5. The judges said that the Jim Crow laws _____.
    - ○ must be stopped
    - ○ were fair to all
    - ○ were not important

© Evan-Moor Corp. • EMC 3202 • Reading Informational Text

Name: _____

SOCIAL STUDIES

Rosa Parks Rides the Bus

I Read Closely

Read the text closely.
Mark the sentence that goes with the picture.

○ Rosa Parks worked as a seamstress.

○ She put on her hat and coat to go home.

○ Rosa Parks quietly said, "No."

○ When the bus came, Rosa Parks got on and sat down.

○ Mrs. Parks was taken to jail.

○ It was her right to sit where she wanted.

○ They rode in cars and taxis together.

○ The judges said the laws were unfair and must be stopped.

Name: _____

SOCIAL STUDIES

Rosa Parks Rides the Bus

Words I Know

Read and answer.

1. He will pay _____ for speeding.
   - ○ an unfair
   - ○ a jail
   - ○ a fine

2. The _____ will fix your torn jacket.
   - ○ seamstress
   - ○ police
   - ○ judge

3. Mom meets us at the _____ after school.
   - ○ bus stop
   - ○ bravely
   - ○ important

4. The last month of the year is _____.
   - ○ Alabama
   - ○ December
   - ○ Montgomery

5. _____ is a state.
   - ○ Montgomery
   - ○ African American
   - ○ Alabama

6. A _____ makes sure laws are fair.
   - ○ bus driver
   - ○ judge
   - ○ seamstress

© Evan-Moor Corp. • EMC 3202 • Reading Informational Text

Name: _____

I Can Write

Look at the pictures.
Write something about Rosa Parks for each one.

_____
_____
_____
_____

_____
_____
_____
_____

_____
_____
_____
_____

SOCIAL STUDIES

Rosa Parks Rides the Bus

60   Reading Informational Text • EMC 3202 • © Evan-Moor Corp.

Name: _____

SOCIAL STUDIES

Rosa Parks Rides the Bus

What I Learned

Write about Rosa Parks.
Tell what she did that changed the lives of African Americans.

_____
_____
_____
_____
_____

Draw a picture about what you wrote.

Social Studies
What Does Congress Do?

Lesson Objective Students will learn what the United States Congress is and how Congress makes new laws.

Content Knowledge The United States has a system of government in which leaders are elected to represent the people. Being a citizen includes having rights and responsibilities as described in the Constitution and laws.

Lesson Preparation

Reproduce and distribute to each student one copy of the dictionary page (p. 65), the student text (p. 66), and the activity pages (pp. 67–71).

Learn

1. Build Background

2. Introduce the Vocabulary
   Dictionary

3. Read the Texts
   What Does Congress Do?
   Teacher's Complex Text

Analyze

4. Reading Comprehension Activities
   I Read and Understand
   I Read Closely

5. Close Reading Activity
   Oral Discussion Questions

6. Vocabulary Activities
   Words I Know

Write

7. Writing Activities
   I Can Write
   What I Learned

1 Build Background

Explain to students that people in a family or a school find ways to get along and work together. How do the members of your family help each other? How do the people in your class take turns? They probably follow rules. Rules help people get along together. Rules for a country are called laws. People in a country need laws. In the United States, people choose leaders to be in a group called Congress. Their job is to make laws that are fair and help run the country.

2 Introduce the Vocabulary

Content Vocabulary Point to each pictured word. Read the word aloud and have students echo you. Then have them write the word on the line. Explain phonetic structures that are unfamiliar to your students. Discuss word meanings as needed. Point out the following:

• There are some words in the text that begin with a capital letter because they are used as proper names: *Capitol, Congress, Constitution*. Explain that when these words are used as common nouns, they begin with a lowercase letter.

Words to Know Point to each word and read it aloud. Have students echo you.

CCSS: RIT 2.1, 2.2, 2.3, 2.4, 2.6, 2.7   W 2.2, 2.8   SL 2.2

3 Read the Texts

Student Text Guide students in reading the text together aloud. Then have them retell the main idea and give details they learned about Congress from the text.

Teacher's Complex Text Have students look at the graphic in their text and listen as you read aloud the Teacher's Complex Text on page 64. Say: *Look at the graphic and listen as I read more information about Congress.*

4 Reading Comprehension Activities

Guide students through completing the activities on pages 67 and 68. Encourage them to look at their text to find information.

5 Close Reading Activity

Oral Discussion Use the Oral Discussion Questions on the right to guide students in a discussion about what they have read and heard. Before you begin, make sure each student has colored pencils and his or her text.

Begin by reading aloud a question and having students answer the question and mark the answer in their text.

6 Vocabulary Activity

Review the vocabulary on the *Dictionary* page. Then guide students through the *Words I Know* activity.

7 Writing Activities

Guide students through the first writing activity, *I Can Write*. Then have them read aloud their lists and sentences to a partner. Discuss the writing prompt on the second writing page, *What I Learned*. As an informal assessment of students' understanding, have them write their responses independently.

Oral Discussion Questions

1. What is the title of this text? (*What Does Congress Do?*) **Draw a green line under it.** Why did the author write the title in the form of a question? (*so we will read on to find out the answer*)

2. What is the Constitution? (*a plan for running the country*) **Draw a yellow line under the sentence that tells the answer.** In what year was it written? (*1787*) **Draw a blue circle around the answer.**

3. What does Congress meet together to do? (*Congress meets together to make laws for the United States.*) **Draw a red line under the sentence.**

4. Look at the graphic at the bottom of the page. Name the three steps that happen before the United States has a new law. (*1. Congress meets to discuss bills. 2. Congress votes. 3. A bill goes to the president to see if he agrees.*) **Draw a purple line under the sentences that tell you.**

5. Which do you think is more fair: to have one person, such as a king, making the laws; or to have a congress chosen by the people making the laws? Why? (*E.g., A congress is more fair, because it represents what the people want, and one person doesn't have all the power.*)

6. How can people have a say in making new laws? (*E.g., People can vote for their leaders in Congress; they can talk to the leaders in Congress if they have a concern or an idea for a new law.*)

Social Studies
Teacher's Complex Text

What Does Congress Do?

People in a country need rules, or laws, so they can get along with each other. Who makes the rules for people in the United States? A group called Congress does. People vote for leaders from their own state to be in Congress. The job of Congress is to make laws for the United States.

Congress knows how to do the job of making laws, because they follow a plan called the Constitution. The Constitution was written in 1787 by our Founding Fathers when the United States became a new country. The Constitution says that the leaders must be chosen by the people, and they must share the power of making laws and running the government. The government is made up of the laws, leaders, and the plan, or system, for running the country.

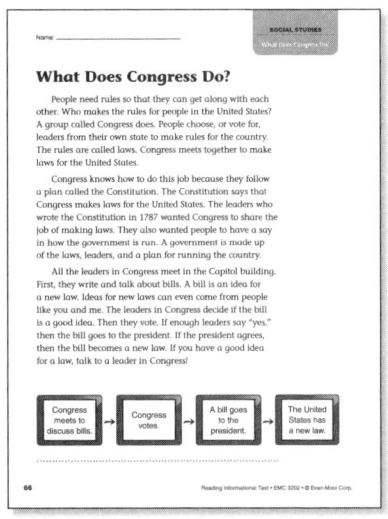

student text, pg. 66

Congress meets in the Capitol building, located in Washington, D.C. The Capitol building is easy to see because it has a huge dome, or round roof, with a statue on top. There are two groups of leaders in Congress, called houses. One group is the Senate, and other group is the House of Representatives. The houses of Congress meet separately. First they meet to write and discuss bills. A bill is an idea for a new law. Sometimes, people have a concern and want to talk to Congress about passing a law. Talking about the bill helps the members of Congress decide if a bill is a good idea. Then both houses of Congress vote. If enough leaders vote "yes" to pass the bill, then it goes to the president. If the president agrees with the bill, then it becomes a new law. If you have a concern or a good idea for a law, you can talk to a member of Congress.

Name: _____

SOCIAL STUDIES
What Does Congress Do?

Dictionary

Look at the picture. Read the word.
Write the word on the line.

Content Vocabulary

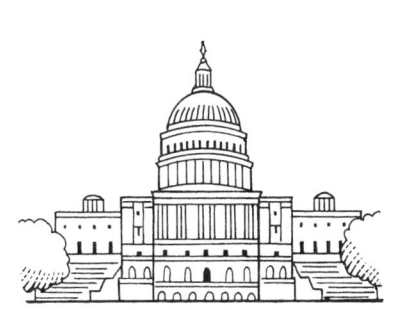
Capitol building
_____

Congress
_____

Constitution
_____

law
_____

United States
_____

vote
_____

Words to Know

| agree | bill | choose | enough |
| government | leaders | president | share |

© Evan-Moor Corp. • EMC 3202 • Reading Informational Text

65

What Does Congress Do?

People need rules so that they can get along with each other. Who makes the rules for people in the United States? A group called Congress does. People choose, or vote for, leaders from their own state to make rules for the country. The rules are called laws. Congress meets together to make laws for the United States.

Congress knows how to do this job because they follow a plan called the Constitution. The Constitution says that Congress makes laws for the United States. The leaders who wrote the Constitution in 1787 wanted Congress to share the job of making laws. They also wanted people to have a say in how the government is run. A government is made up of the laws, leaders, and a plan for running the country.

All the leaders in Congress meet in the Capitol building. First, they write and talk about bills. A bill is an idea for a new law. Ideas for new laws can even come from people like you and me. The leaders in Congress decide if the bill is a good idea. Then they vote. If enough leaders say "yes," then the bill goes to the president. If the president agrees, then the bill becomes a new law. If you have a good idea for a law, talk to a leader in Congress!

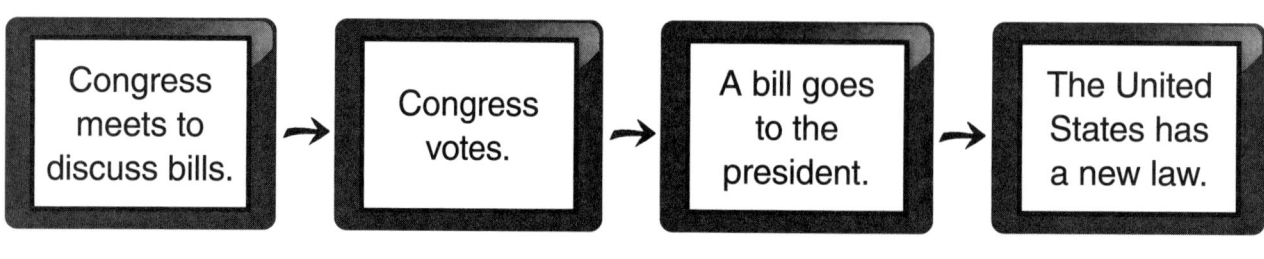

Name: _____

SOCIAL STUDIES
What Does Congress Do?

I Read and Understand

Read and answer.

1. The Constitution is _____.
    - ○ a vote
    - ○ a president
    - ○ a plan

2. People in the United States _____.
    - ○ can't have ideas for laws
    - ○ choose who will make laws
    - ○ do not have a say in the government

3. Congress talks about a bill _____.
    - ○ after the president agrees
    - ○ before they vote on it
    - ○ before they meet

4. The Constitution was written in _____.
    - ○ 1787
    - ○ 1987
    - ○ 2007

5. Congress meets in _____.
    - ○ the Capitol building
    - ○ each state
    - ○ every country

Name: _____

I Read Closely

Read the text closely.
Finish the sentence. You can use words from the text.

Constitution

1. The Constitution of the United States says that Congress _____
_____

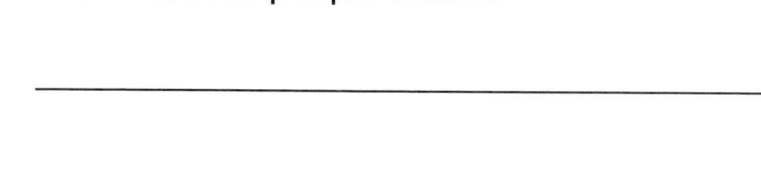
vote

2. The American people choose _____
_____

Congress

3. The leaders who make the laws meet _____
_____

bill

4. The leaders in Congress decide _____
_____

Name: _____

SOCIAL STUDIES
What Does Congress Do?

Words I Know

Read and answer.

1. We will _____ for the best leader.
   - ○ bill
   - ○ share
   - ○ vote

2. A _____ is an idea for a new law.
   - ○ rule
   - ○ bill
   - ○ choose

3. The _____ building has a round roof.
   - ○ Capitol
   - ○ Congress
   - ○ Constitution

4. To say **yes** to something is to _____.
   - ○ enough
   - ○ share
   - ○ agree

5. A rule for a country is a _____.
   - ○ law
   - ○ vote
   - ○ leader

6. If the _____ agrees, the bill becomes law.
   - ○ leader
   - ○ choose
   - ○ president

© Evan-Moor Corp. • EMC 3202 • Reading Informational Text

Name: _____

I Can Write

Read the phrases in the box.
Write the phrases that tell what Congress does in order.

What Does Congress Do?

- writes the bill
- meets in the Capitol building
- meets in the Constitution
- does not share the job
- talks about the bill
- votes on the bill

Congress:

1. _____

2. _____

3. _____

4. _____

Write a sentence to answer each question.

1. What does the Constitution tell Congress to do?

_____

_____

2. What happens if the president agrees with the bill?

_____

Name: _____

SOCIAL STUDIES

What Does Congress Do?

What I Learned

Write about Congress.
Tell what Congress is. Tell what Congress does.
Use the list you made to help.

_____

_____

_____

_____

_____

_____

_____

_____

_____

_____

_____

_____

Biography
Ben Franklin and the Glass Harmonica

Lesson Objective Students will learn how Benjamin Franklin was not only a leader, but also a person of many other talents. They will become familiar with one of his inventions: the glass harmonica.

Content Knowledge People of the past made a difference for others. We can learn about ourselves by acquiring deeper insights into their lives.

Lesson Preparation

Reproduce and distribute to each student one copy of the dictionary page (p. 75), the student text (p. 76), and the activity pages (pp. 77–81).

Learn

1. Build Background
2. Introduce the Vocabulary
   Dictionary
3. Read the Texts
   Ben Franklin and the Glass Harmonica
   Teacher's Complex Text

Analyze

4. Reading Comprehension Activities
   I Read and Understand
   I Read Closely
5. Close Reading Activity
   Oral Discussion Questions
6. Vocabulary Activity
   Words I Know

Write

7. Writing Activities
   I Can Write
   What I Learned

1 Build Background

Explain that Benjamin Franklin lived long ago when America was a new country. Franklin was one of the Founding Fathers—one of America's first great leaders. He signed the Declaration of Independence. He is famous for many other things. He flew a kite in a lightning storm to find out about electricity. He wrote and printed books and newspapers. These are just a few of his many accomplishments.

2 Introduce the Vocabulary

Content Vocabulary Point to each pictured word. Read the word aloud and have students echo you. Then have them write the word on the line. Explain word structures that are new to your students. For example, point out the two different sounds that /c/ makes in *concert*. Discuss word meanings as needed.

Words to Know Point to each word and read it aloud. Have students echo you. Point out the following:

- The word *museum* has the same beginning as *musician*.
- The word *harmonica* comes from a very old word that means "musical."
- A glass harmonica is a large instrument.

CCSS: RIT 2.1, 2.2, 2.3, 2.4, 2.6, 2.7   W 2.2, 2.8   SL 2.2

3 Read the Texts

Student Text Guide students in reading the text together aloud. Then have them retell the main idea and give details they learned about Benjamin Franklin's glass harmonica from the text.

Teacher's Complex Text Have students look at the picture in their text and listen as you read aloud the Teacher's Complex Text on page 74. Say: *Look at the picture and listen as I read more information about Ben Franklin and his glass harmonica invention.*

4 Reading Comprehension Activities

Guide students through completing the activities on pages 77 and 78. Encourage them to look at their text to find information.

5 Close Reading Activity

Oral Discussion Use the Oral Discussion Questions on the right to guide students in a discussion about what they have read and heard. Before you begin, make sure each student has colored pencils and his or her text.

Begin by reading aloud a question. Then have students answer the question and mark the answer in their text.

6 Vocabulary Activity

Review the vocabulary on the *Dictionary* page. Then guide students through the *Words I Know* activity.

7 Writing Activities

Guide students through the first writing activity, *I Can Write*. Then have them read aloud their sentences to a partner. Discuss the writing prompt on the second writing page, *What I Learned*. As an assessment of students' understanding of the topic, have them write their responses independently.

Oral Discussion Questions

1. **What is the title of the text?** (*Ben Franklin and the Glass Harmonica*) **Draw a blue line under it.**

2. **What did the title make you wonder about?** (*E.g., Who is Ben Franklin? What is a glass harmonica?*) **What does a good title do?** (*E.g., A title makes you wonder what you will read about and helps you think about the topic.*)

3. **Name some jobs Ben Franklin did.** (*He was one of America's first leaders. He was also a writer, printer, scientist, musician, and inventor.*) **Draw an orange line under the words that name each job.**

4. **Which paragraph describes a glass harmonica?** (*paragraph 2*) **Make a red X beside it. How would you describe a glass harmonica to someone? Look at the picture to help you.** (*E.g., The glass harmonica had glass bowls that turned on a rod. The player turned the rod using a foot pedal and played the bowls with wet fingers.*)

5. **What does the author think was a reason the glass harmonica stopped being used as much?** (*It was harder to hear the soft sounds of the glass harmonica in new, large concert halls.*) **Make a green dot next to each sentence that tells about it.**

6. **How do you know that this text is a biography?** (*It tells about Ben Franklin's life.*)

© Evan-Moor Corp. • EMC 3202 • Reading Informational Text

Ben Franklin and the Glass Harmonica

Ben Franklin was a famous American and one of our country's first leaders. He signed the Declaration of Independence in 1776, which declared America free from British rule. He was a Founding Father who helped write the United States Constitution in 1787. Ben was a person with many talents and interests. He was an author, printer, scientist, musician, and an inventor, too!

Ben Franklin traveled to England and France many times. On one of his visits to England, he heard a man play music on the rims of glasses filled with water. Music was one of Ben's great interests, and this gave him an idea. In 1761, he invented a glass harmonica. It was made of glass bowls of different sizes that turned on a rod. By turning the rod with a foot pedal, the bowls spun around. Then, using wet fingers, he would play music on the edges of the bowls.

Ben Franklin gave concerts with his glass harmonica, and it became quite popular. Other musicians took up playing the instrument. Even the queen of France, Marie Antoinette, learned to play it. Famous composers such as Wolfgang Amadeus Mozart and Ludwig van Beethoven composed music to be played on the glass harmonica. Soon, newer, larger concert halls began to change musical concerts. Music had been played in smaller rooms, mostly in palaces, for the rich. Now it came to be played in larger spaces, where common people could enjoy it. The soft, light sound of the glass harmonica was more difficult to hear, and after a time it went out of style. Today, these instruments are mostly found in museums. However, some people still enjoy listening to and playing the glass harmonica.

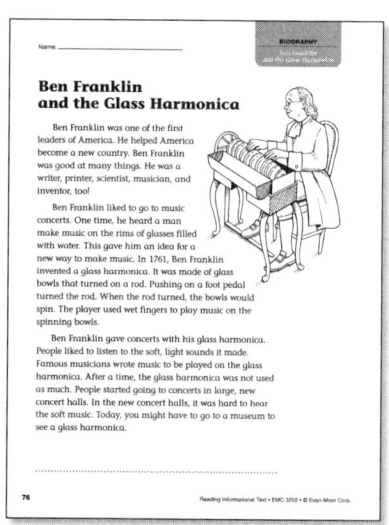

student text, pg. 76

Name: _____

> BIOGRAPHY
> Ben Franklin and the Glass Harmonica

Dictionary

Look at the picture. Read the word.
Write the word on the line.

Content Vocabulary

Ben Franklin

_____

bowl

_____

concert

_____

glass harmonica

_____

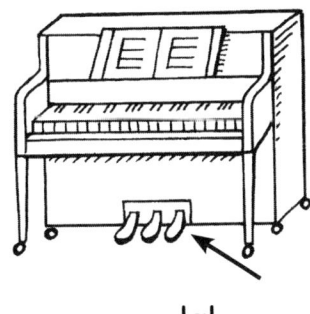

pedal

_____

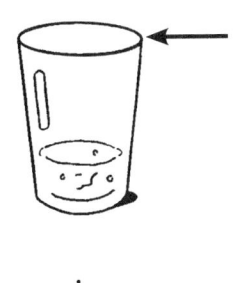

rim

_____

Words to Know

America	country	famous	fingers
inventor	museum	musician	printer
scientist	writer		

© Evan-Moor Corp. • EMC 3202 • Reading Informational Text

75

Name: _____

Ben Franklin and the Glass Harmonica

Ben Franklin was one of the first leaders of America. He helped America become a new country. Ben Franklin was good at many things. He was a writer, printer, scientist, musician, and inventor, too!

Ben Franklin liked to go to music concerts. One time, he heard a man make music on the rims of glasses filled with water. This gave him an idea for a new way to make music. In 1761, Ben Franklin invented a glass harmonica. It was made of glass bowls that turned on a rod. Pushing on a foot pedal turned the rod. When the rod turned, the bowls would spin. The player used wet fingers to play music on the spinning bowls.

Ben Franklin gave concerts with his glass harmonica. People liked to listen to the soft, light sounds it made. Famous musicians wrote music to be played on the glass harmonica. After a time, the glass harmonica was not used as much. People started going to concerts in large, new concert halls. In the new concert halls, it was hard to hear the soft music. Today, you might have to go to a museum to see a glass harmonica.

BIOGRAPHY
Ben Franklin and the Glass Harmonica

Name: _____

BIOGRAPHY

Ben Franklin and the Glass Harmonica

I Read and Understand

Read and answer.

1. Ben Franklin helped _____ become a country.
   - ○ a musician
   - ○ America
   - ○ a concert

2. A glass harmonica _____.
   - ○ plays music
   - ○ prints books
   - ○ makes glass

3. A glass harmonica has _____.
   - ○ keys
   - ○ strings
   - ○ bowls

4. A glass harmonica sounds _____.
   - ○ loud and bright
   - ○ soft and light
   - ○ strong and fast

5. Ben Franklin's glass harmonica was invented in _____.
   - ○ 1761
   - ○ 1861
   - ○ 1961

Name: _____

BIOGRAPHY

Ben Franklin and the Glass Harmonica

I Read Closely

Read the text closely.
Mark the sentence that goes with the picture.

- ○ Ben Franklin invented a glass harmonica.
- ○ Ben Franklin was one of the first leaders of America.

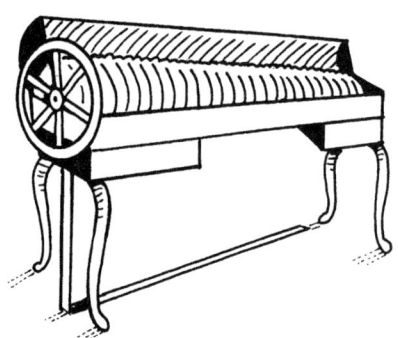

- ○ The harmonica had glass bowls that turned on a rod.
- ○ Ben Franklin was interested in many different things.

- ○ Today, glass harmonicas are found mostly in museums.
- ○ Ben Franklin gave concerts with his glass harmonica.

- ○ Music played on glass rims gave Ben Franklin an idea.
- ○ A foot pedal turned the rod and the bowls.

78 Reading Informational Text • EMC 3202 • © Evan-Moor Corp.

Name: _____

BIOGRAPHY

Ben Franklin and the Glass Harmonica

Words I Know

Read and answer.

1. A person who makes something using a new idea is _____.
   - ○ an inventor
   - ○ a musician
   - ○ a writer

2. Fill the glass to the _____.
   - ○ bowl
   - ○ rim
   - ○ pedal

3. A harmonica player is _____.
   - ○ a scientist
   - ○ a writer
   - ○ a musician

4. A lot of people know about a _____ person.
   - ○ famous
   - ○ printer
   - ○ museum

5. Put your foot on the _____.
   - ○ fingers
   - ○ bowl
   - ○ pedal

6. We heard a _____ at school.
   - ○ rim
   - ○ pedal
   - ○ concert

© Evan-Moor Corp. • EMC 3202 • Reading Informational Text

Name: _____

BIOGRAPHY

Ben Franklin and the Glass Harmonica

I Can Write

Look at the pictures.
Write something about Ben Franklin for each one.

leader

_____
_____
_____

glass harmonica

_____
_____
_____

concert

_____
_____
_____

Name: _____

BIOGRAPHY

Ben Franklin and the Glass Harmonica

What I Learned

1. Explain how Ben Franklin got the idea for the glass harmonica.

   _____
   _____
   _____
   _____
   _____

2. Describe Ben Franklin's glass harmonica.

   _____
   _____
   _____
   _____
   _____

Biography
Thank You, Sarah Josepha Hale

Lesson Objective Students will learn how Sarah Josepha Hale helped to influence the creation of a Thanksgiving Day national holiday.

Content Knowledge Celebrations are significant to understanding how people in history have helped shape the nation.

Lesson Preparation

Reproduce and distribute to each student one copy of the dictionary page (p. 85), the student text (p. 86), and the activity pages (pp. 87–91).

Learn

1. Build Background

2. Introduce the Vocabulary
   Dictionary

3. Read the Texts
   Thank you, Sarah Josepha Hale
   Teacher's Complex Text

Analyze

4. Reading Comprehension Activities
   I Read and Understand
   I Read Closely

5. Close Reading Activity
   Oral Discussion Questions

6. Vocabulary Activity
   Words I Know

Write

7. Writing Activities
   I Can Write
   What I Learned

1 Build Background

Explain to students that the first Thanksgiving was held in 1621 in Plymouth. About 140 English Pilgrims and Wampanoag joined in a feast together. The Pilgrims were grateful they had survived their first year in America, with the help of the native people. They feasted on a harvest of corn, beans, and squash. These were foods the Wampanoag had taught the Pilgrims to grow. They hunted geese, duck, and deer for the feast. Fish and eel were also on the menu. The first Thanksgiving lasted for several days.

2 Introduce the Vocabulary

Content Vocabulary Point to each pictured word. Read the word aloud and have students echo you. Then have them write the word on the line. Explain phonetic structures that are unfamiliar to your students. Point out the following:

- Words ending in *e* often drop the *e* when *–ing* is added. For example, the word *battle* becomes *battling*. The word *give* becomes *giving* (in *Thanksgiving*).

Words to Know Point to each word and read it aloud. Have students echo you. Explain that *tastes* is a multiple-meaning word. Tell students that in this text, *tastes* means "people's likes and dislikes."

CCSS: RIT 2.1, 2.2, 2.3, 2.4, 2.6, 2.7   W 2.2, 2.8   SL 2.2

3 Read the Texts

Student Text Guide students in reading the text together aloud. Then have them retell the main idea and give details they learned about Sarah Josepha Hale from the text.

Teacher's Complex Text Have students look at the picture in their text and listen as you read aloud the Teacher's Complex Text on page 84. Say: *Look at the picture and listen as I read more information about Sarah Josepha Hale.*

4 Reading Comprehension Activities

Guide students through completing the activities on pages 87 and 88. Encourage them to look at their text to find information.

5 Close Reading Activity

Oral Discussion Use the Oral Discussion Questions on the right to guide students in a discussion about what they have read and heard. Before you begin, make sure each student has colored pencils and his or her text.

Begin by reading aloud a question. Then have students answer the question and mark the answer in their text.

6 Vocabulary Activity

Review the vocabulary on the *Dictionary* page. Then guide students through the *Words I Know* activity.

7 Writing Activities

Guide students through the first writing activity, *I Can Write*. Have them read their timelines with a partner. Discuss the writing prompt on the second writing page, *What I Learned*. As an informal assessment of students' understanding, have them write their paragraphs independently.

Oral Discussion Questions

1. **What did Sarah Josepha Hale have to do with Thanksgiving?** (*She thought there should be a national Thanksgiving holiday. Her letter convinced President Lincoln to make Thanksgiving a holiday.*) **In what year did Abraham Lincoln make Thanksgiving Day a holiday for the whole country?** (*1863*) **Draw a blue circle around the year.**

2. **What did Sarah Josepha Hale do after her husband died?** (*She became a writer and editor.*) **How can you tell she was good at her work?** (*Many people read the magazine. She shaped America's thinking and tastes.*) **Make a red X next to the paragraph that tells about it.** (*paragraph 2*)

3. **How do you know Sarah Josepha Hale did not give up?** (*For 17 years, Sarah wrote letters to five presidents.*) **Draw a yellow line under the sentence.**

4. **Why did President Lincoln think it was a good time to establish one Thanksgiving Day for all?** (*The states were battling each other in a terrible war. President Lincoln wanted the country to stay together.*) **Draw a brown line under the sentences that tell you.**

5. **What did President Lincoln mean when he said he wanted Americans to give thanks "with one heart and voice?"** (*He wanted Americans to say it together and with feeling.*)

6. **What happened first? Did Sarah Hale become an editor or did Abraham Lincoln receive her letter?** (*Sarah Hale became an editor.*) **Draw a green line under the year it happened.** (*1828*)

Biography
Teacher's Complex Text

Thank You, Sarah Josepha Hale

America celebrates Thanksgiving Day on the last Thursday of November each year. We can thank Sarah Josepha Hale for that. She was born in 1788, was educated at home, and became a schoolteacher when she was a young woman. Later, she married David Hale and they had five children. When her husband died, she needed to support her family, so she became a writer and an editor. Sarah wrote fiction books and poetry. Some of her poems were written for children. You may have heard her poem "Mary's Lamb." Today, we know it as the children's song "Mary Had a Little Lamb."

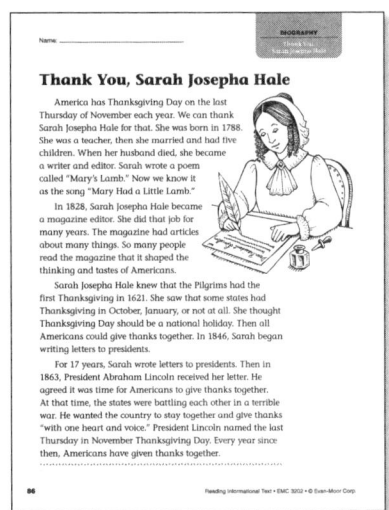

student text, pg. 86

In 1828, Sarah Josepha Hale was asked to be the editor of a magazine for women. The magazine was the *Ladies' Magazine*, later called *Godey's Lady's Book*. Many important writers wrote articles for the magazine, including Nathaniel Hawthorne and Harriet Beecher Stowe. Sarah used her power as an editor and writer. She included many topics varying from fashion to education. So many people read the magazine that it shaped many Americans' thinking and tastes.

Sarah Josepha Hale felt that Thanksgiving should be a holiday celebrated by all Americans. The Pilgrims had held the first Thanksgiving in 1621. There had been many different Thanksgivings after that. Some states had Thanksgiving Day in October. Some celebrated it in January. Many states didn't have a Thanksgiving Day at all. In 1846, Sarah wrote a letter to the president. She asked for a Thanksgiving Day to be held on the same day in all the states—a national holiday. It would be a day for all Americans to give thanks together.

For 17 years, Sarah wrote letters to different presidents about creating a national Thanksgiving Day. Sarah didn't give up. In 1863, President Abraham Lincoln received a letter from Sarah Josepha Hale. He agreed it was time for Americans to give thanks together. The states were battling each other in a terrible civil war. President Lincoln wanted the country to stay together. He wanted Americans to give thanks "with one heart and voice." He did as Sarah suggested. President Lincoln signed a proclamation saying that Thanksgiving Day would be a national holiday on the last Thursday in November. Every year since then, Americans have given thanks together on Thanksgiving Day.

Name: _____

BIOGRAPHY
Thank You, Sarah Josepha Hale

Dictionary

Look at the picture. Read the word.
Write the word on the line.

Content Vocabulary

battling
_____

magazine
_____

Pilgrims
_____

president
_____

teacher
_____

Thanksgiving
_____

Words to Know

Abraham Lincoln	agree	America	articles
editor	married	national	poem
tastes	voice	writer	

Thank You, Sarah Josepha Hale

America has Thanksgiving Day on the last Thursday of November each year. We can thank Sarah Josepha Hale for that. She was born in 1788. She was a teacher, then she married and had five children. When her husband died, she became a writer and editor. Sarah wrote a poem called "Mary's Lamb." Now we know it as the song "Mary Had a Little Lamb."

In 1828, Sarah Josepha Hale became a magazine editor. She did that job for many years. The magazine had articles about many things. So many people read the magazine that it shaped the thinking and tastes of Americans.

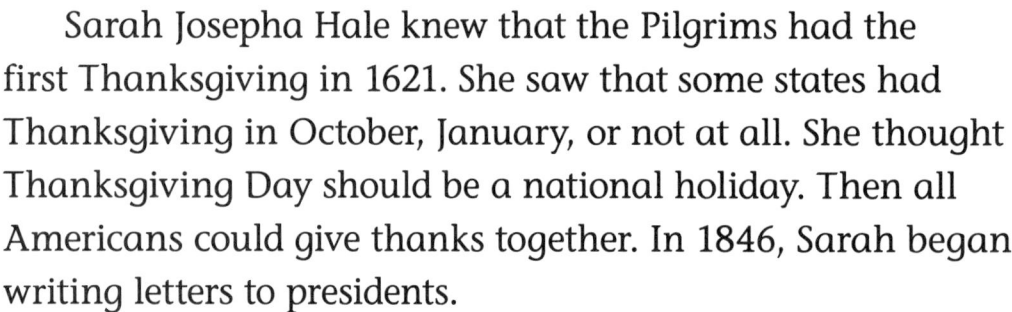

Sarah Josepha Hale knew that the Pilgrims had the first Thanksgiving in 1621. She saw that some states had Thanksgiving in October, January, or not at all. She thought Thanksgiving Day should be a national holiday. Then all Americans could give thanks together. In 1846, Sarah began writing letters to presidents.

For 17 years, Sarah wrote letters to presidents. Then in 1863, President Abraham Lincoln received her letter. He agreed it was time for Americans to give thanks together. At that time, the states were battling each other in a terrible war. He wanted the country to stay together and give thanks "with one heart and voice." President Lincoln named the last Thursday in November Thanksgiving Day. Every year since then, Americans have given thanks together.

Name: _____

BIOGRAPHY
Thank You, Sarah Josepha Hale

I Read and Understand

Read and answer.

1. Sarah Josepha Hale wrote a poem called ____.
   - ○ "Thanksgiving Day"
   - ○ "Mary's Lamb"
   - ○ "The Pilgrims"

2. Sarah Josepha Hale wanted to have Thanksgiving on ____.
   - ○ many different days
   - ○ President Lincoln's birthday
   - ○ the same day everywhere

3. Sarah Josepha Hale did not give up ____.
   - ○ writing letters
   - ○ her magazine job
   - ○ battling the states

4. Lincoln wanted the country ____.
   - ○ not to have Thanksgiving at all
   - ○ to stay together
   - ○ to write letters to Sarah Hale

5. Thanksgiving Day is in ____ every year.
   - ○ January
   - ○ October
   - ○ November

Name: _____

BIOGRAPHY

Thank You, Sarah Josepha Hale

I Read Closely

Read the text closely.
Finish the sentence with the words used in the text.

Thanksgiving

1. America has Thanksgiving Day on
_____
_____

editor

2. In 1828, Sarah Josepha Hale became
_____
_____

"Mary's Lamb"

3. Sarah Josepha Hale wrote _____
_____
_____

Lincoln

4. He wanted the country to stay together and
_____
_____

Name: _____

> **BIOGRAPHY**
> Thank You, Sarah Josepha Hale

Words I Know

Read and answer.

1. We give thanks on _____ Day.
    - ○ Pilgrims
    - ○ Thanksgiving
    - ○ National

2. _____ means "fighting."
    - ○ National
    - ○ Battling
    - ○ Agree

3. I like to read articles in a _____.
    - ○ magazine
    - ○ poem
    - ○ voice

4. The _____ came to live in America.
    - ○ editor
    - ○ articles
    - ○ Pilgrims

5. Abraham Lincoln was a _____.
    - ○ president
    - ○ writer
    - ○ teacher

6. _____ decides what will be in a magazine.
    - ○ A president
    - ○ A teacher
    - ○ An editor

Name: _____

BIOGRAPHY

Thank You, Sarah Josepha Hale

I Can Write

A timeline shows the order in which things happened.
Fill in the timeline about Sarah Josepha Hale and Thanksgiving Day.

Timeline: Sarah Josepha Hale

Year	What Happened?
1621	_____
1788	_____
1828	_____
1846	_____
1863	_____

Name: _____

BIOGRAPHY
Thank You, Sarah Josepha Hale

What I Learned

Write about the life of Sarah Josepha Hale.
Tell about the things she did. Use the timeline you made.

_____

_____

_____

_____

_____

_____

_____

_____

_____

_____

_____

_____

_____

How-to
Fun with Magnets

Lesson Objective Students will learn that magnetic forces can pull objects that contain iron or steel.

Content Knowledge Magnetic forces vary in strength, are attracted to iron and steel, and can pull through some materials.

Lesson Preparation

Reproduce and distribute to each student one copy of the dictionary page (p. 95), the student text (p. 96), and the activity pages (pp. 97–101).

Learn

1. Build Background

2. Introduce the Vocabulary
   Dictionary

3. Read the Texts
   Fun with Magnets
   Teacher's Complex Text

Analyze

4. Reading Comprehension Activities
   I Read and Understand
   I Read Closely

5. Close Reading Activity
   Oral Discussion Questions

6. Vocabulary Activity
   Words I Know

Write

7. Writing Activities
   I Can Write
   What I Learned

1 Build Background

Explain that there are many kinds of rocks. Some rocks can attract or pull pieces of iron. Scientists call these rocks *magnetic*. Scientists think some rocks may become magnetic from being struck by lightning. Magnetic rocks are used to make magnets, which are used in many ways.

2 Introduce the Vocabulary

Content Vocabulary Point to each pictured word. Read the word aloud and have students echo you. Then have them write the word on the line. Explain phonetic structures that are unfamiliar to your students. Point out the following:

- The words *beehive* and *shoebox* are compound words.

Words to Know Point to each word and read it aloud. Have students echo you. Explain word meanings as needed. Point out the following:

- In this text, the word *object* means "goal or purpose."

- The word *stronger* ends with *-er*. Explain that *stronger* means "more strong."

CCSS: RIT 2.1, 2.2, 2.3, 2.4, 2.6, 2.7   W 2.2, 2.8   SL 2.2

3 Read the Texts

Student Text Guide students in reading the text together aloud. Then have them retell the main idea and give details they learned about magnets from the text.

Teacher's Complex Text Have students look at the pictures in their text and listen as you read aloud the Teacher's Complex Text on page 94. Say: *Look at the pictures and listen as I read more information about magnets.*

4 Reading Comprehension Activities

Guide students through completing the activities on pages 97 and 98. Encourage them to look at their text to find information.

5 Close Reading Activity

Oral Discussion Use the Oral Discussion Questions on the right to guide students in a discussion about what they have read and heard. Before you begin, make sure each student has colored pencils and his or her text.

Begin by reading aloud a question. Then have students answer the question and mark the answer in their text.

6 Vocabulary Activity

Review the vocabulary on the *Dictionary* page. Then guide students through the *Words I Know* activity.

7 Writing Activities

Guide students through the first writing activity, *I Can Write*. Then have them read aloud their graphic organizers to a partner. Discuss the writing prompt on the second writing page, *What I Learned*. As an informal assessment of students' understanding, have them write their paragraphs independently. Optional: Have students make the magnet game.

Oral Discussion Questions

1. What is the title of this text? (*Fun with Magnets*) **Draw a green line under the title.**

2. Why do you think the author included an activity in the text? (*The author wanted students to have a fun way to see how magnets pull toward objects made with iron or steel, and to see that if the force is strong enough, it can go through some materials.*) **Draw a blue line under the sentences that tell how to test your magnet.**

3. What is the activity in the text called? (*"Make a Magnet Game"*) **Draw a purple line under the title for the activity.**

4. What was the author's purpose for writing the first paragraph? (*The author wanted students to get ready for the activity by learning some facts, wondering about how magnets work, and gathering supplies to test a magnet's force.*) **Make an orange X next to that paragraph.**

5. Read number 2 in the directions. Why do you think you would draw a path with loops and turns? (*E.g., A path with loops and turns is more challenging and fun than a straight path.*) **Make a yellow X by the sentence that gives directions about this.**

6. Can you describe the purpose of a "how-to" text? (*A how-to text tells how to do or make something step by step.*) Why did the author include pictures? (*The pictures help you see what to do for each step.*)

How-to
Teacher's Complex Text

Fun with Magnets

We know that magnets have a force even though the force is invisible, or can't be seen. How do we know this invisible force exists? We can see what a magnet's force does. It attracts, or pulls, things that are made of iron, nickel, or cobalt. Steel is an example of a metal that is mixed with iron. A magnet's force is also attracted to steel. Some things magnets attract are needles, iron nails, and some refrigerator doors. Magnets have forces of different strengths. Stronger magnets can pull or move heavier objects. How can you test the force? Make a game to see a magnet's force at work. You will need a shoebox lid. You will also need paper, scissors, tape, colored pens, a metal paper clip, and a strong magnet.

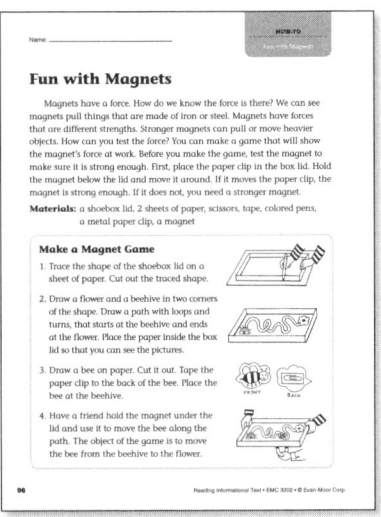
student text, pg. 96

Test the magnet to see if it is strong enough to attract through the cardboard lid. To do this, place a metal paper clip in the box lid. Hold up the lid, flat. Move the magnet under the lid to see if the magnet will move the paper clip. Does it move the paper clip? If it does, then it is strong enough to play the game. If it does not, you can test other magnets. When you find a magnet that is strong enough, you are ready to begin.

Make a Magnet Game

1. Put the box lid on the paper. Draw around it. Then cut out the shape and trim it to fit inside the box lid. Remove the paper.

2. Draw a flower in one corner of the paper. Draw a beehive in another corner. Draw a path from the flower to the beehive. Design your path with loops and some turns. Place the paper back in the box lid.

3. Draw and cut out a bee from a scrap of paper. Tape the paper clip to the back of the bee.

4. To play the game, you can hold up the lid and have a friend hold the magnet under the lid. Place the bee on the beehive. Have your friend move the bee along the path. Can he or she make the bee go from the beehive to the flower and back?

Name: _____

HOW-TO

Fun with Magnets

Dictionary

Look at the picture. Read the word.
Write the word on the line.

Content Vocabulary

beehive

_____

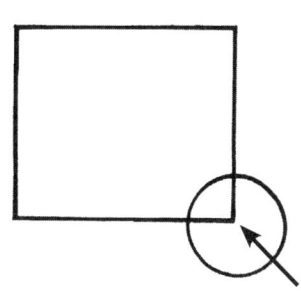

corner

_____

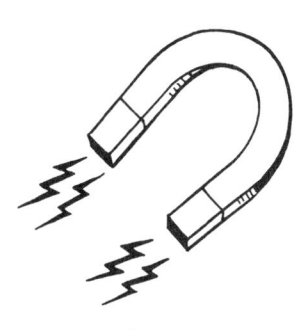

force

_____

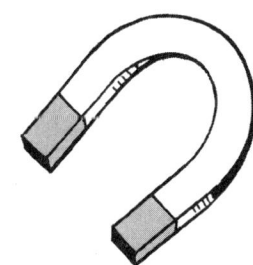

magnet

_____

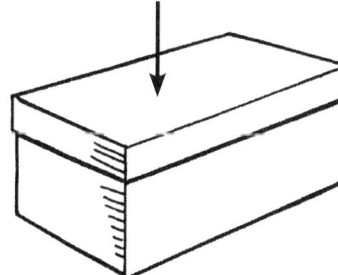

shoebox lid

_____

strength

_____

Words to Know

| enough | iron | loop | metal |
| object | scissors | steel | stronger |

© Evan-Moor Corp. • EMC 3202 • Reading Informational Text   95

Name: _____

HOW-TO

Fun with Magnets

Fun with Magnets

Magnets have a force. How do we know the force is there? We can see magnets pull things that are made of iron or steel. Magnets have forces that are different strengths. Stronger magnets can pull or move heavier objects. How can you test the force? You can make a game that will show the magnet's force at work. Before you make the game, test the magnet to make sure it is strong enough. First, place the paper clip in the box lid. Hold the magnet below the lid and move it around. If it moves the paper clip, the magnet is strong enough. If it does not, you need a stronger magnet.

Materials: a shoebox lid, 2 sheets of paper, scissors, tape, colored pens, a metal paper clip, a magnet

Make a Magnet Game

1. Trace the shape of the shoebox lid on a sheet of paper. Cut out the traced shape.

2. Draw a flower and a beehive in two corners of the shape. Draw a path with loops and turns, that starts at the beehive and ends at the flower. Place the paper inside the box lid so that you can see the pictures.

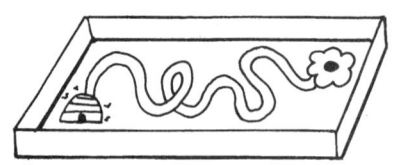

3. Draw a bee on paper. Cut it out. Tape the paper clip to the back of the bee. Place the bee at the beehive.

FRONT   BACK

4. Have a friend hold the magnet under the lid and use it to move the bee along the path. The object of the game is to move the bee from the beehive to the flower.

Name: _____

> HOW-TO
>
> Fun with Magnets

I Read and Understand

Read and answer.

1. A magnet's force _____.
   - ○ is easy to see
   - ○ is always strong
   - ○ pulls objects made of iron

2. Magnets _____.
   - ○ have different strengths
   - ○ cut through paper clips
   - ○ pick up paper

3. A magnet's force can move through _____.
   - ○ a beehive
   - ○ a flower
   - ○ a shoebox lid

4. Use a lid and a magnet to _____.
   - ○ test paper
   - ○ make a game
   - ○ make a flower

5. What is taped to the paper bee?
   - ○ a paper clip
   - ○ a corner
   - ○ a magnet

Name: _____

HOW-TO

Fun with Magnets

I Read Closely

Read the text closely.
Finish the sentence with the words used in the text.

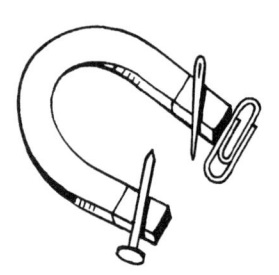

1. We can see magnets _____
   _____
   _____

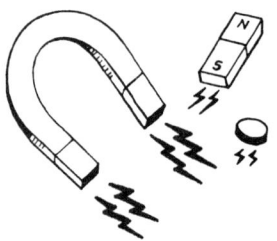

2. Magnets have forces _____
   _____
   _____

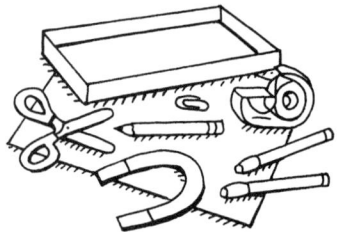

3. You can make a _____
   _____
   _____

4. Tape the paper clip _____
   _____
   _____

Name: _____

HOW-TO

Fun with Magnets

Words I Know

Read and answer.

1. A _____ lid has four corners.
   - ○ magnet
   - ○ shoebox
   - ○ steel

2. Iron and steel are kinds of _____.
   - ○ loop
   - ○ metal
   - ○ tape

3. The _____ magnet can pull more.
   - ○ strength
   - ○ corner
   - ○ stronger

4. A magnet's _____ pulls a paper clip.
   - ○ object
   - ○ beehive
   - ○ force

5. I hear the bees buzz in the _____.
   - ○ beehive
   - ○ steel
   - ○ loop

6. Use _____ to cut the paper.
   - ○ enough
   - ○ scissors
   - ○ magnets

© Evan-Moor Corp. • EMC 3202 • Reading Informational Text

Name: _____

HOW-TO

Fun with Magnets

I Can Write

Write four facts about magnets.

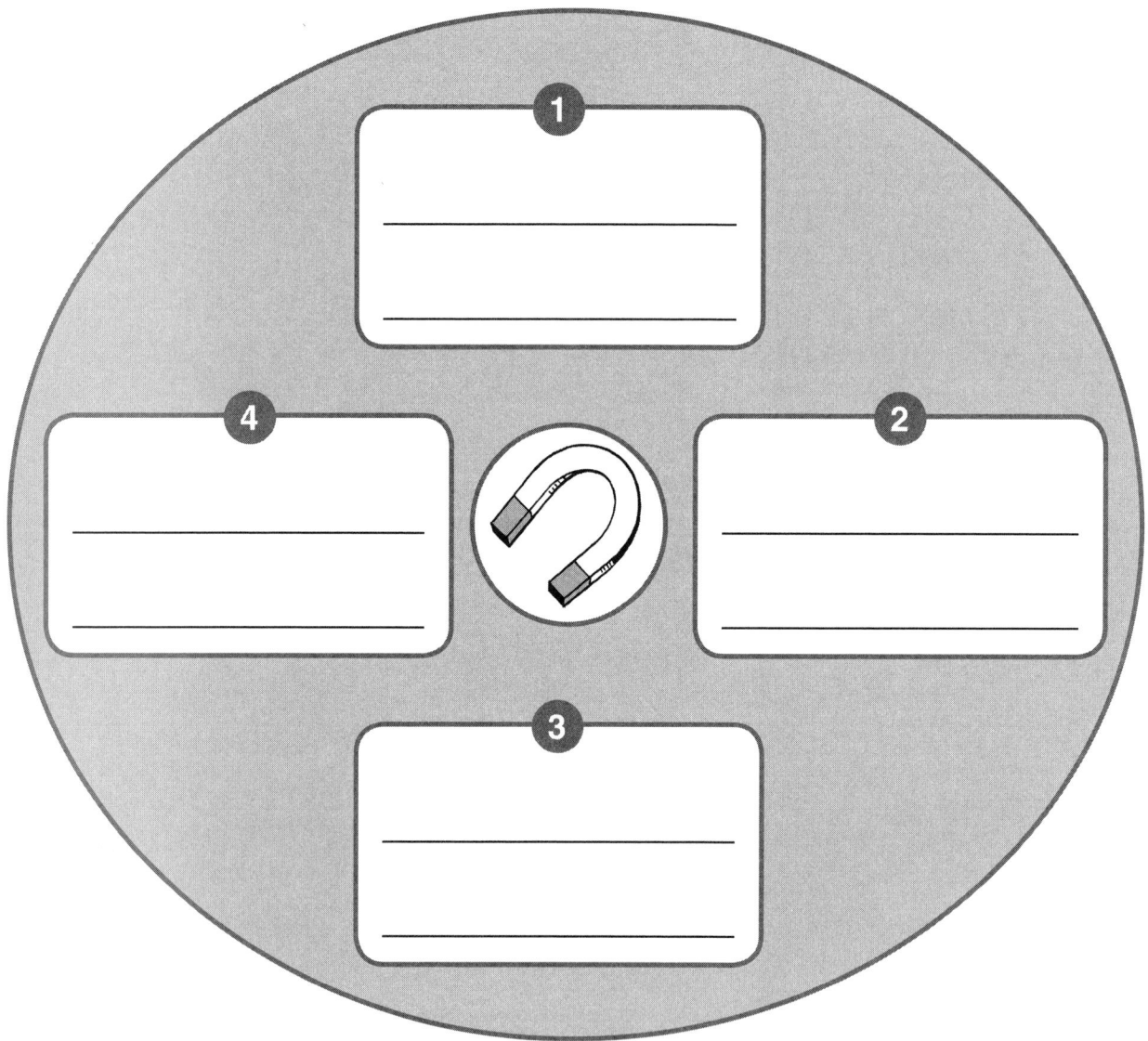

Can the paper bee move without the paper clip?
Write a sentence to tell why or why not.

_____

_____

Name: _____

What I Learned

Look at the picture. Write a paragraph about the magnet game. Explain how the bee moves from the beehive to the flower.

_____
_____
_____
_____

Write a paragraph that tells why the magnet should be tested first.

_____
_____
_____
_____

Technical
Help Wanted: Earth Engineer

Lesson Objective Students will learn that geology is the study of Earth's soil and rocks. They will also learn that an earth engineer works to take care of the earth and keep people safe.

Content Knowledge There are many careers in the fields of science and technology. A career in geological engineering is one that involves taking care of the environment and ensuring quality of life for people.

Lesson Preparation

Reproduce and distribute to each student one copy of the dictionary page (p. 105), the student text (p. 106), and the activity pages (pp. 107–111).

Learn

1. Build Background

2. Introduce the Vocabulary
   Dictionary

3. Read the Texts
   Help Wanted: Earth Engineer
   Teacher's Complex Text

Analyze

4. Reading Comprehension Activities
   I Read and Understand
   I Read Closely

5. Close Reading Activity
   Oral Discussion Questions

6. Vocabulary Activity
   Words I Know

Write

7. Writing Activities
   I Can Write
   What I Learned

1 Build Background

Explain to students that many people enjoy rock collecting. They like to identify, or figure out, what kind of rock they are looking at. They notice details about the rock: how it looks, how it feels, where it was found. People who collect rocks can learn a lot about the earth.

2 Introduce the Vocabulary

Content Vocabulary Point to each pictured word. Read the word aloud and have students echo you. Then have them write the word on the line. Explain phonetic structures that are unfamiliar to your students. Point out the following:

- *Coal* is a black rock that is mined (dug) from the ground and used as fuel.
- A *dam* is a barrier that is built across a stream, river, or lake to hold back water.
- The word *Earth* with a capital *E* is the name for the planet we live on.
- The word *earth* with a lowercase *e* means the land, soil, and rocks.

Words to Know Point to each word and read it aloud. Have students echo you. Explain that *copper, gold, salt,* and *diamonds* are also types of rocks found in the earth.

CCSS: RIT 2.1, 2.2, 2.3, 2.4, 2.6, 2.7   W 2.2, 2.8   SL 2.2

3 Read the Texts

Student Text Guide students in reading the text together aloud. Then have them retell the main idea and give details they learned about earth engineers from the text.

Teacher's Complex Text Have students look at the picture in their text and listen as you read aloud the Teacher's Complex Text on page 104. Say: *Look at the picture and listen as I read more information about earth engineers.*

4 Reading Comprehension Activities

Guide students through completing the activities on pages 107 and 108. Encourage them to look at their text to find information.

5 Close Reading Activity

Oral Discussion Use the Oral Discussion Questions on the right to guide students in a discussion about what they have read and heard. Before you begin, make sure each student has colored pencils and his or her text.

Begin by reading aloud a question. Then have students answer the question and mark the answer in their text.

6 Vocabulary Activity

Review the vocabulary on the *Dictionary* page. Then guide students through the *Words I Know* activity.

7 Writing Activities

Guide students through the first writing activity, *I Can Write*. Then have them read aloud and discuss their sentences with a partner. Discuss the writing prompt in the second writing activity, *What I Learned*. As an informal assessment of students' understanding, have them write and illustrate their paragraphs independently.

Oral Discussion Questions

1. Name a job or career that might interest people who like rocks. (*earth engineer*) Why? (*An earth engineer studies and works with the earth and rocks.*) Draw a red line under the name of the career.

2. What are some examples of work that earth engineers might do? (*build dams, tunnels, roads, buildings*) Make a purple X by the paragraph that tells you. (*paragraph 2*)

3. The meaning of the word *geology* comes from its two parts. *Geo-* means "earth" and *–ology* means "the study of." So, geology is the study of Earth. Draw a blue line under the sentence that tells the meaning of *geology*. (*The study of Earth and its rocks is called* geology.)

4. Name some rocks an earth engineer might help find. (*copper, gold, salt, coal, diamonds*) Draw an orange line under each rock name.

5. Reread paragraph 3. Name two places where earth engineers do their work. (*Earth engineers work outdoors and in a lab.*) Circle each place with brown. Which place does the picture show earth engineers working? (*outdoors*)

6. What was the author's purpose in writing this text? (*The author wanted us to learn about how to become an earth engineer, and what earth engineers do.*)

Technical
Teacher's Complex Text

Help Wanted: Earth Engineer

Do you like to look at rocks? There are many kinds of rocks. You can find them everywhere. In fact, Earth is a giant ball of rock. The study of Earth and its rocks is called *geology*.

If you like learning about rocks, you may want to be a geological engineer someday. Another name for a geological engineer is an *earth engineer*. To become an earth engineer, a person goes to college to study both geology and engineering. In geology, the person learns about the earth and what rocks are made of. An earth engineer also learns how to design things such as tunnels, bridges, roadways, and dams. He or she studies the ways in which the soil and rocks will affect these structures. Earth engineers also learn how to take care of the earth in mining operations (digging for rocks), and how to keep people safe from earthquakes, floods, and volcanoes.

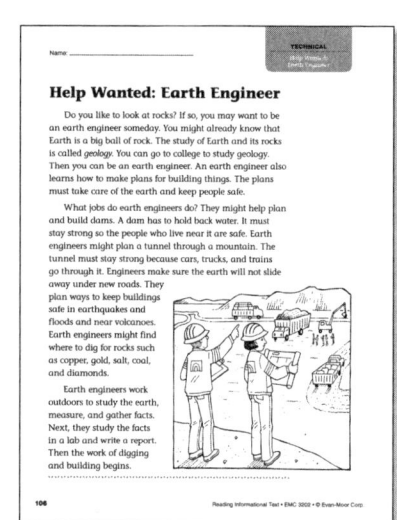

student text, pg. 106

What jobs do earth engineers do? They might help design and build dams. A dam has to hold back water, and it must stay strong so the people who live near it are safe. The earth around a dam must be carefully studied to be sure it will hold. Earth engineers might also help design a tunnel through a mountain. The tunnel must stay strong because cars, trucks, and trains move through it all the time. Earth engineers study how to blast through rock. Engineers make sure the earth will not slide away under new roads and highways. They plan ways to keep buildings safe by studying earthquakes, floods, and volcanoes. Earth engineers might work for a mining company. A mining company digs up minerals and metals such as copper, iron, gold, salt, coal, and diamonds. Engineers help a mining company discover where to dig.

You might think an earth engineer works outdoors all the time. It is a good job for a person who likes being out in nature. However, only part of the time is spent outdoors. The earth engineer studies the earth at the work site. He or she takes measurements, makes observations, and gathers data. Then the engineer studies the data in a lab and writes a report. After that, the work of digging and building begins.

Name: _____

TECHNICAL

Help Wanted:
Earth Engineer

Dictionary

Look at the picture. Read the word.
Write the word on the line.

Content Vocabulary

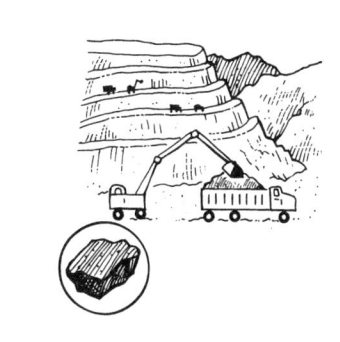

coal

_____

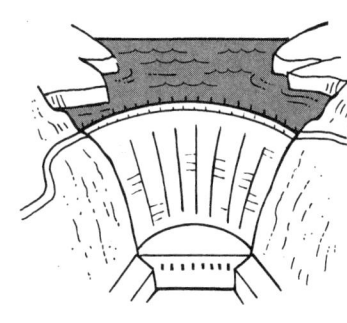

dam

_____

earthquake

_____

lab

_____

tunnel

_____

volcano

_____

Words to Know

building	college	copper	diamonds
engineer	flood	geology	gold
measure	mountain	salt	

Help Wanted: Earth Engineer

Do you like to look at rocks? If so, you may want to be an earth engineer someday. You might already know that Earth is a big ball of rock. The study of Earth and its rocks is called *geology*. You can go to college to study geology. Then you can be an earth engineer. An earth engineer also learns how to make plans for building things. The plans must take care of the earth and keep people safe.

What jobs do earth engineers do? They might help plan and build dams. A dam has to hold back water. It must stay strong so the people who live near it are safe. Earth engineers might plan a tunnel through a mountain. The tunnel must stay strong because cars, trucks, and trains go through it. Engineers make sure the earth will not slide away under new roads. They plan ways to keep buildings safe in earthquakes and floods and near volcanoes. Earth engineers might find where to dig for rocks such as copper, gold, salt, coal, and diamonds.

Earth engineers work outdoors to study the earth, measure, and gather facts. Next, they study the facts in a lab and write a report. Then the work of digging and building begins.

Name: _____

TECHNICAL

Help Wanted:
Earth Engineer

I Read and Understand

Read and answer.

1. Geology is the study of _____.
   - ○ dams and tunnels
   - ○ cars and trucks
   - ○ earth and rocks

2. Earth engineers might help _____.
   - ○ study the stars
   - ○ plan a tunnel through a mountain
   - ○ find a new way to use salt

3. Earth engineers might look for _____.
   - ○ old buildings
   - ○ where to dig for copper
   - ○ cars and trucks

4. After studying the facts, an engineer _____.
   - ○ writes a report
   - ○ works outdoors
   - ○ enjoys nature

5. Learn about rocks if you want to _____.
   - ○ go through a tunnel
   - ○ drive a train
   - ○ be an earth engineer

Name: _____

TECHNICAL

Help Wanted:
Earth Engineer

I Read Closely

Read the text closely.
Finish the sentence with the words used in the text.

Earth

1. You might already know that _____
_____
_____

tunnel

2. Earth engineers might plan _____
_____
_____

road

3. Engineers make sure the earth will not _____
_____
_____

plans

4. They might help _____
_____
_____

Name: _____

TECHNICAL

Help Wanted:
Earth Engineer

Words I Know

Read and answer.

1. _____ and diamonds are rocks.
   - ○ Buildings
   - ○ Salt
   - ○ Earthquakes

2. A _____ is built to hold back water.
   - ○ dam
   - ○ lab
   - ○ flood

3. A _____ is a mountain with a big hole.
   - ○ geology
   - ○ volcano
   - ○ college

4. _____ is a place to learn.
   - ○ Tunnel
   - ○ Copper
   - ○ College

5. Cars and trucks go through _____.
   - ○ an earthquake
   - ○ a volcano
   - ○ a tunnel

6. A person who plans and builds is _____.
   - ○ an engineer
   - ○ a lab
   - ○ a college

© Evan-Moor Corp. • EMC 3202 • Reading Informational Text

Name: _____

	TECHNICAL
	Help Wanted: Earth Engineer

I Can Write

Look at the pictures.
Write a fact about earth engineers for each one.

_____
_____
_____
_____

_____
_____
_____
_____

_____
_____
_____
_____

110   Reading Informational Text • EMC 3202 • © Evan-Moor Corp.

Name: _____

TECHNICAL

Help Wanted:
Earth Engineer

What I Learned

Write about earth engineers. Tell about some of the jobs they do.

_____

_____

_____

_____

Draw a picture of an earth engineer at work.

Answer Key

TE = Teacher's Edition
SB = Student Book

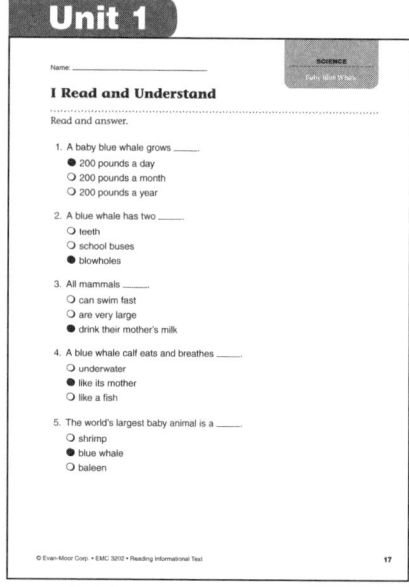

TE Page 17 / SB Page 4

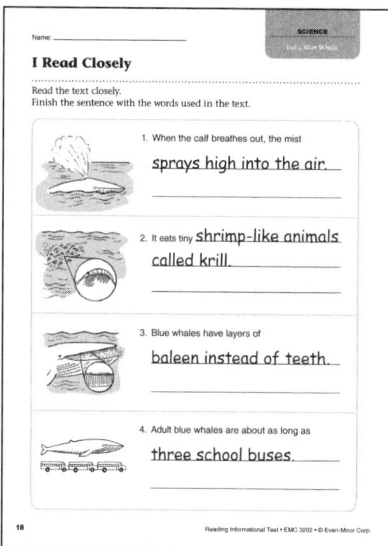

TE Page 18 / SB Page 5

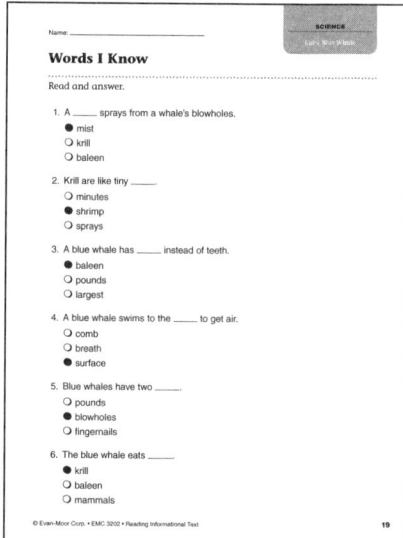

TE Page 19 / SB Page 6

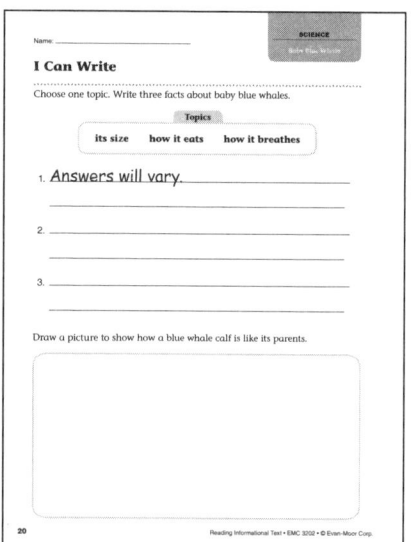

TE Page 20 / SB Page 7

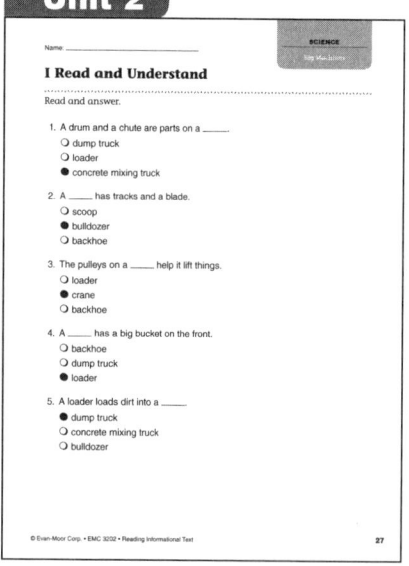

TE Page 27 / SB Page 12

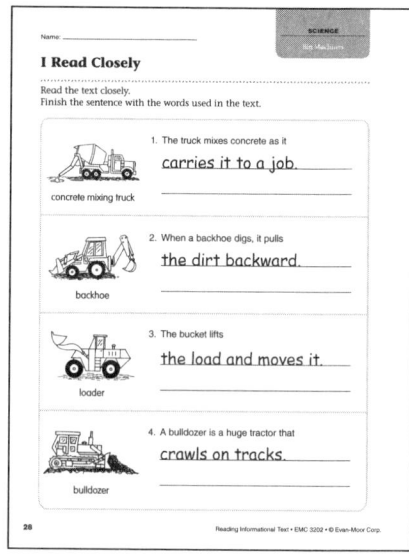

TE Page 28 / SB Page 13

Answer Key

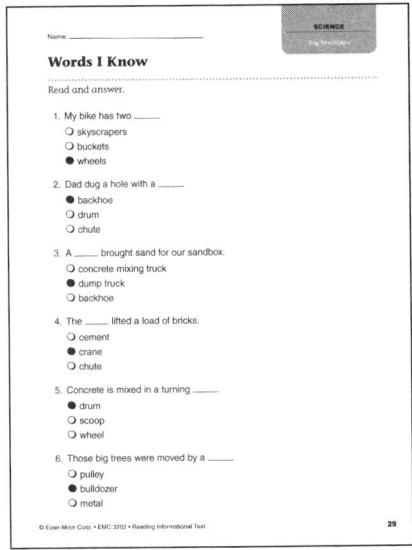
TE Page 29 / SB Page 14

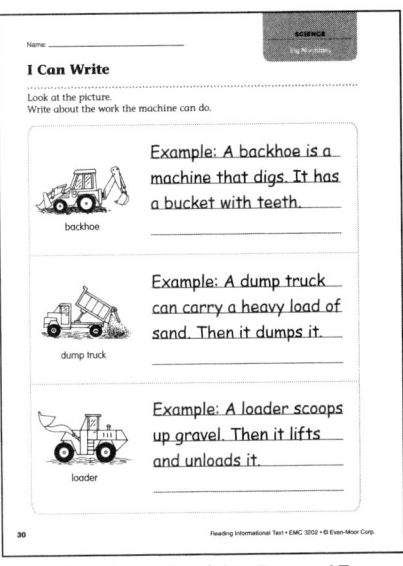
TE Page 30 / SB Page 15

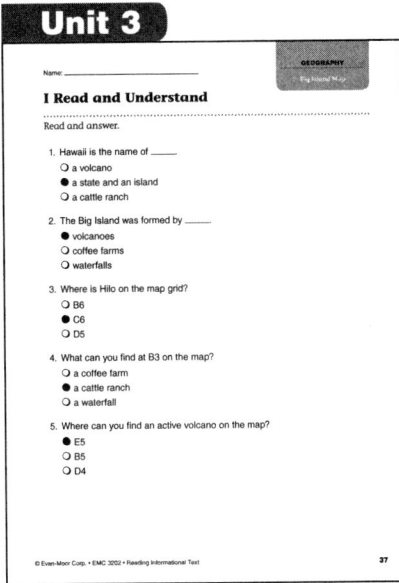
TE Page 37 / SB Page 20

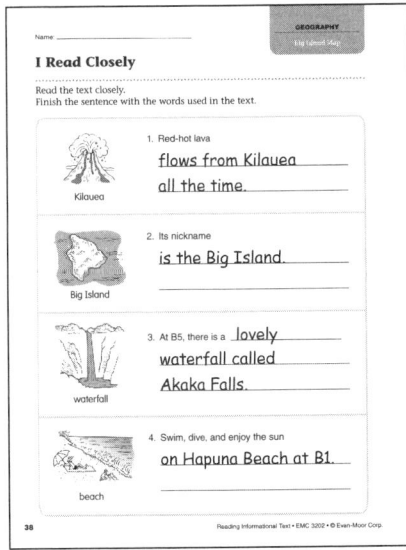
TE Page 38 / SB Page 21

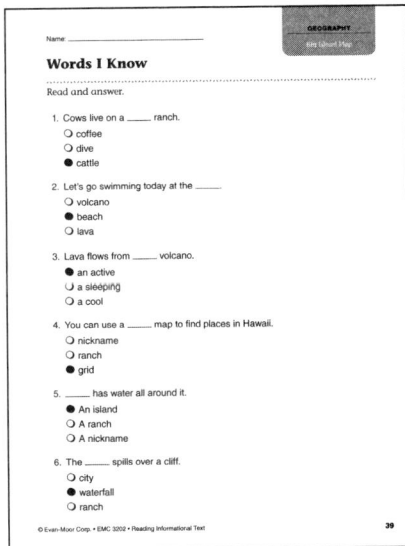
TE Page 39 / SB Page 22

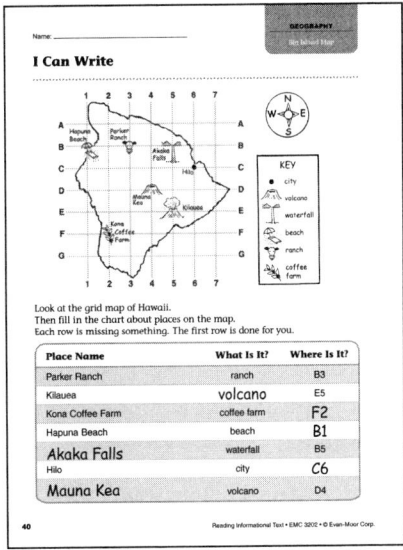
TE Page 40 / SB Page 23

Answer Key

Unit 4

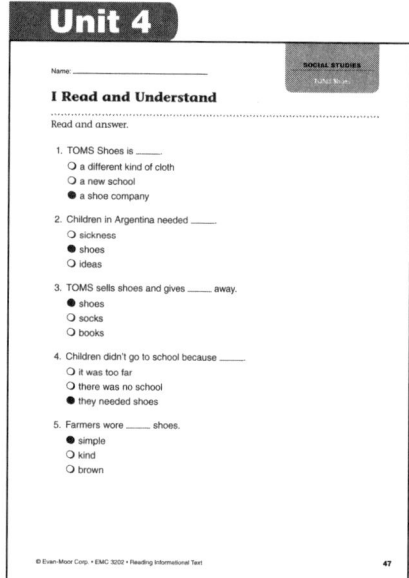
TE Page 47 / SB Page 28

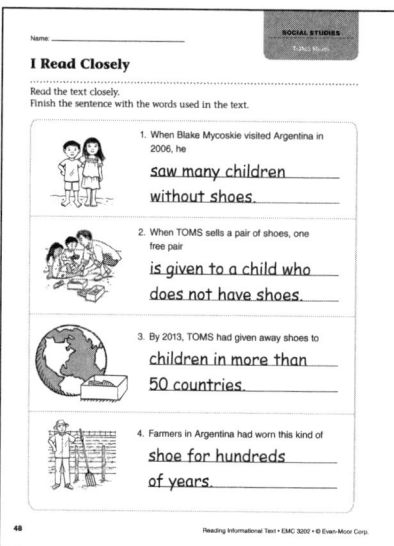
TE Page 48 / SB Page 29

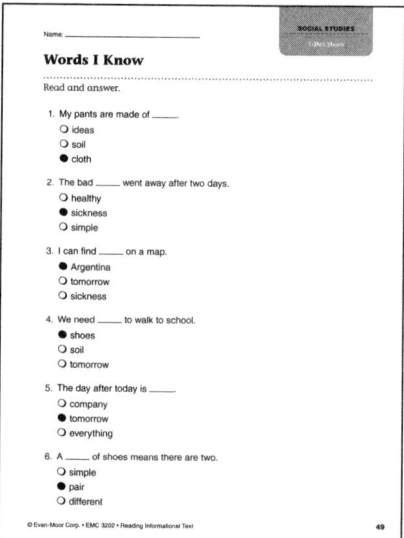
TE Page 49 / SB Page 30

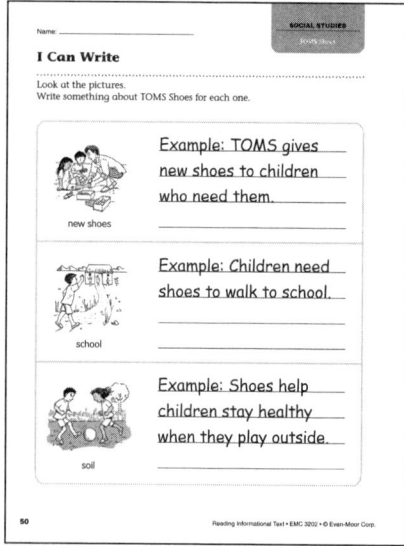
TE Page 50 / SB Page 31

Unit 5

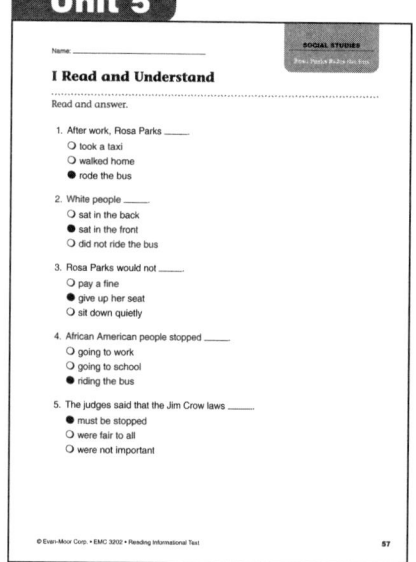
TE Page 57 / SB Page 36

TE Page 58 / SB Page 37

Answer Key

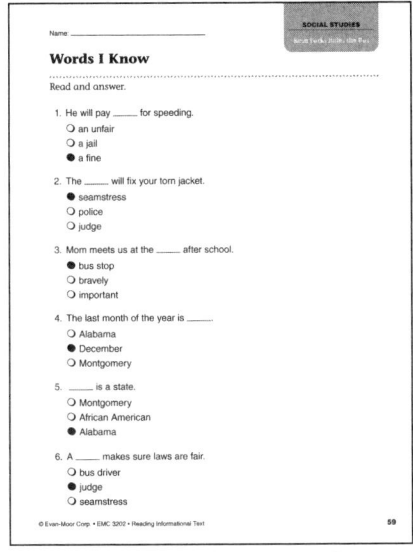

TE Page 59 / SB Page 38

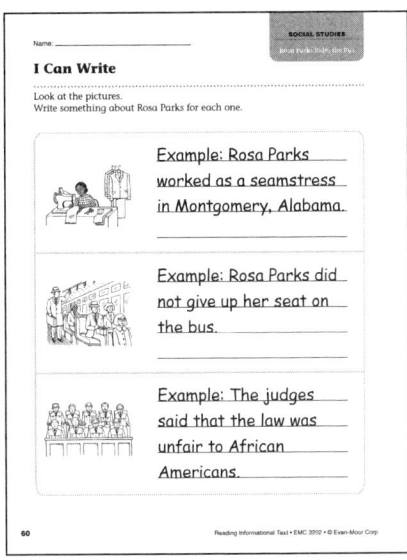

TE Page 60 / SB Page 39

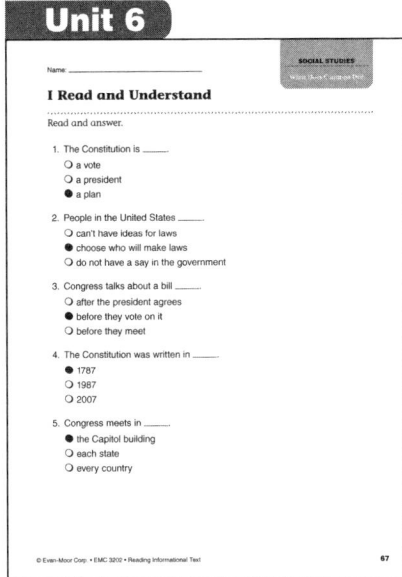

TE Page 67 / SB Page 44

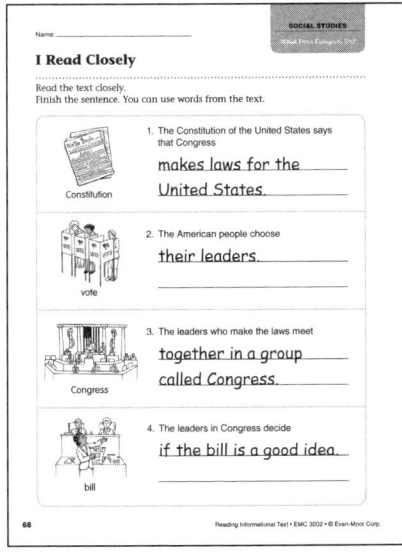

TE Page 68 / SB Page 45

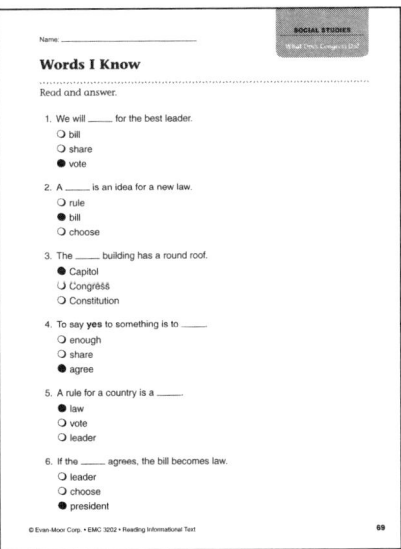

TE Page 69 / SB Page 46

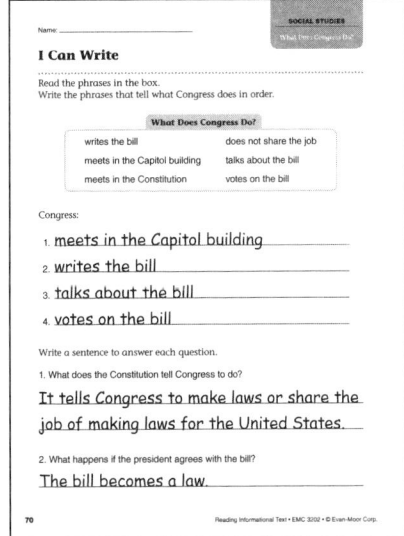

TE Page 70 / SB Page 47

Answer Key

Unit 7

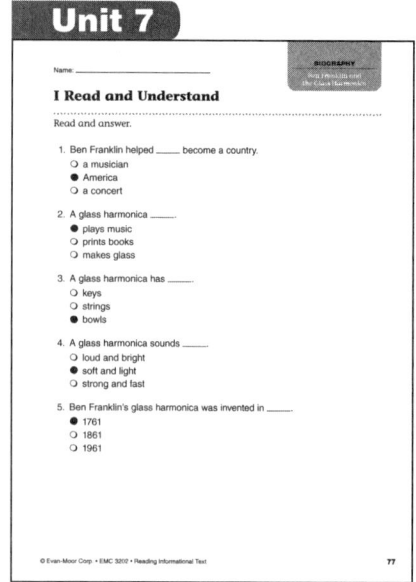
TE Page 77 / SB Page 52

TE Page 78 / SB Page 53

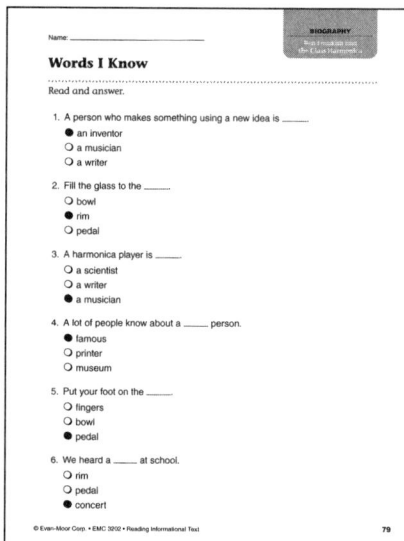
TE Page 79 / SB Page 54

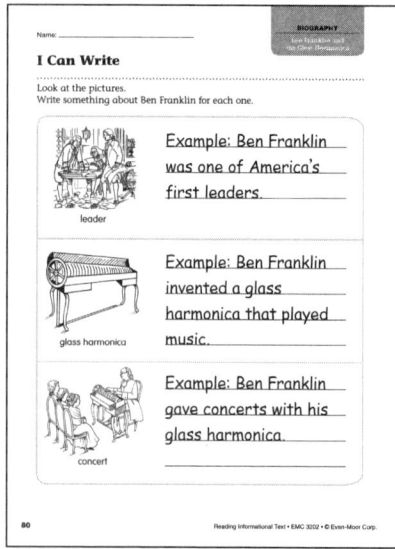
TE Page 80 / SB Page 55

Unit 8

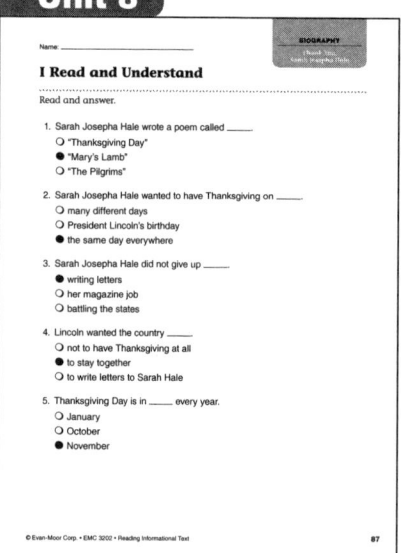
TE Page 87 / SB Page 60

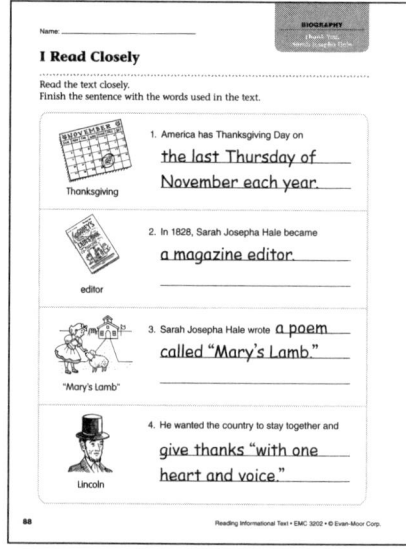
TE Page 88 / SB Page 61

Answer Key

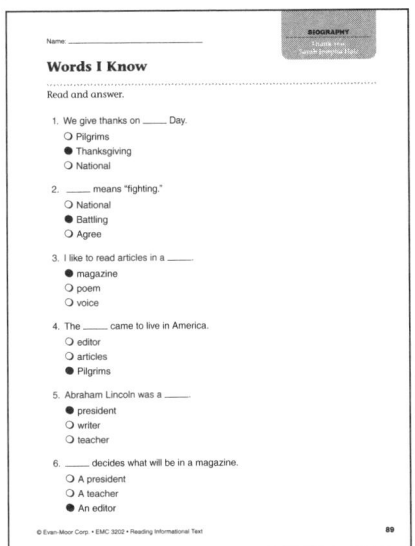

TE Page 89 / SB Page 62

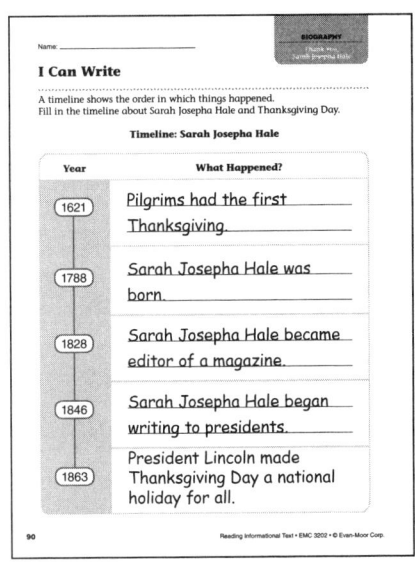

TE Page 90 / SB Page 63

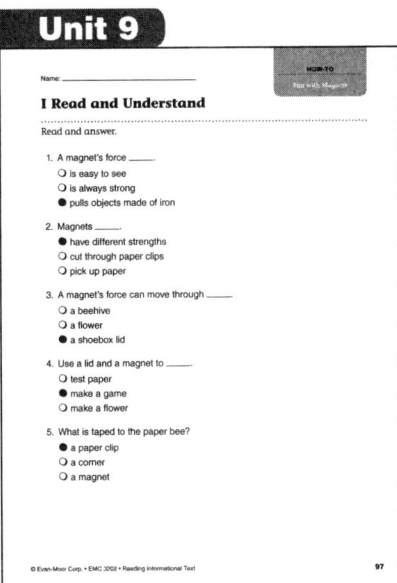

TE Page 97 / SB Page 68

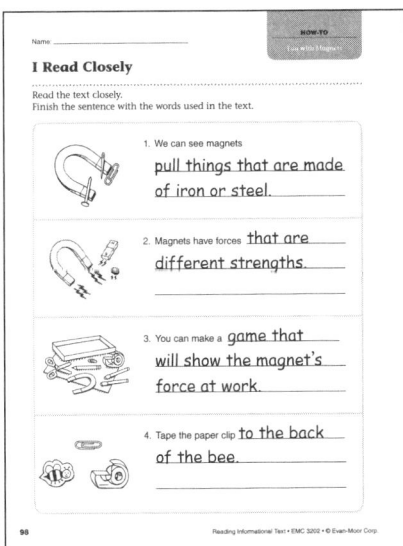

TE Page 98 / SB Page 69

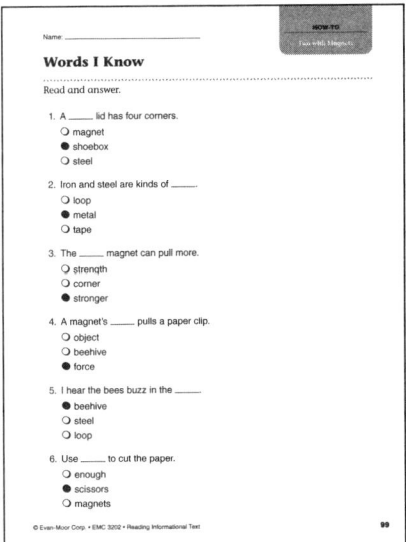

TE Page 99 / SB Page 70

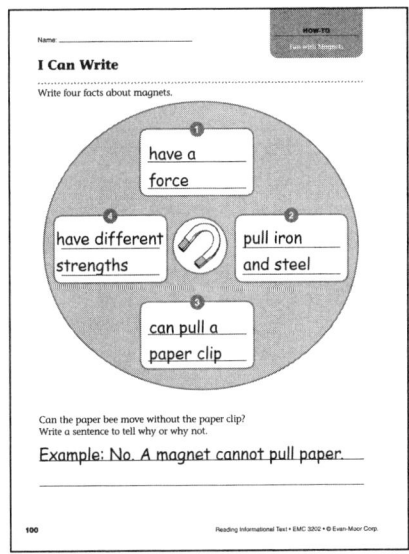

TE Page 100 / SB Page 71

Answer Key

Unit 10

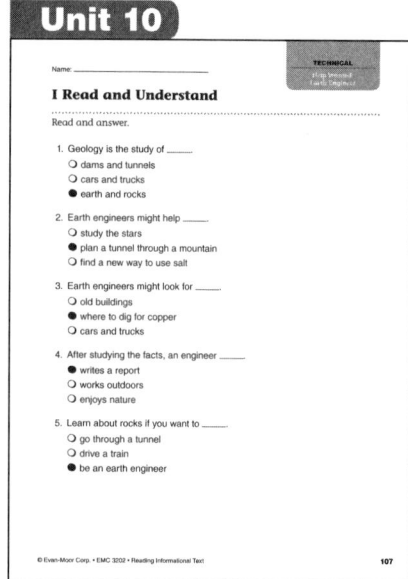
TE Page 107 / SB Page 76

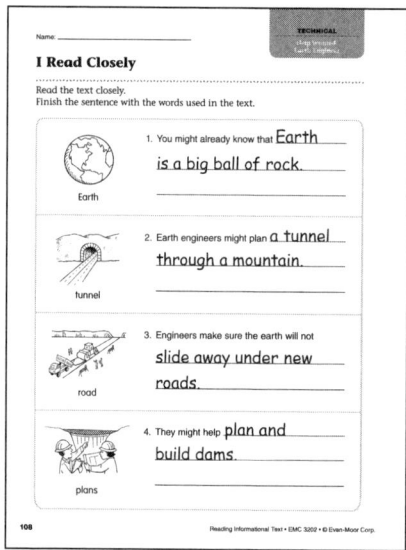
TE Page 108 / SB Page 77

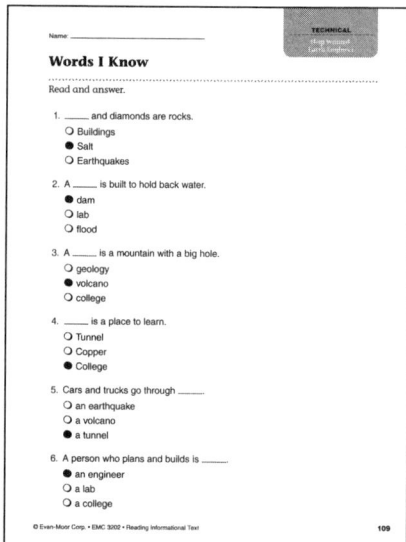
TE Page 109 / SB Page 78

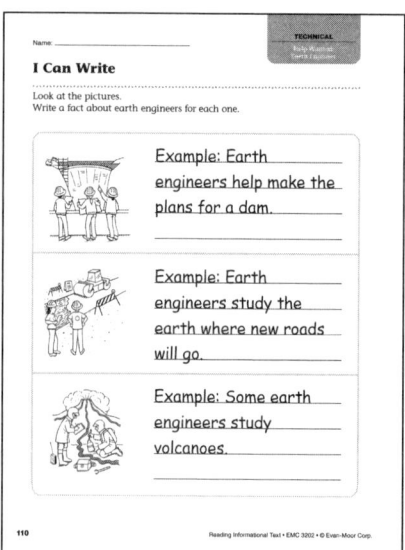
TE Page 110 / SB Page 79

Common Core Lessons
Text-Based Writing Nonfiction
Grade 2

SAMPLER

UNIT 2
Science Article – Level L
Compare-and-Contrast Writing Prompt

Owl Facts

Lesson Objectives

Writing
Students use information from the science article to write a compare-and-contrast paragraph.

Vocabulary
Students learn content vocabulary words and use those words to write about how owls are alike and different.

Content Knowledge
Students understand the unique characteristics of snowy owls and barn owls.

Essential Understanding
Students understand what owls look like and how they live and act in nature.

Prepare

Reproduce and distribute one copy for each student.

	LESSON	PAGE
1	Unit Focus and Lesson Checklist	20
2	Learn Vocabulary	21
3	Read the Science Article: *Owl Facts*	22
4	Answer Questions About the Science Article	23
5	Organize Information	24
6	Write a Compare-and-Contrast Paragraph	25

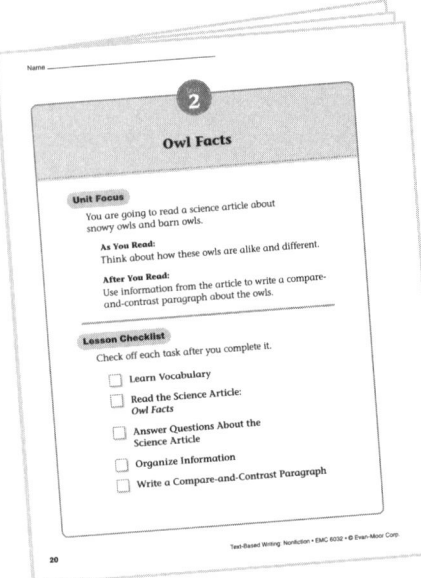

1 **Unit Focus and Lesson Checklist**
Distribute one unit to each student and direct students' attention to the Unit Focus and Lesson Checklist. Tell them they will be able to refer to the focus of the unit as needed while working on the lessons. Instruct students to check off each task on the checklist after they complete it.

Read aloud the focus statements, and verify that students understand their purpose for reading. Ask:

• What are we going to read about? (snowy owls and barn owls)

• What are you going to learn about them? (how they are alike and different)

• What are you going to write based on this article? (a compare-and-contrast paragraph)

CCSS: **W** 2.2, 2.7, 2.8   **RIT** 2.4, 2.5, 2.10

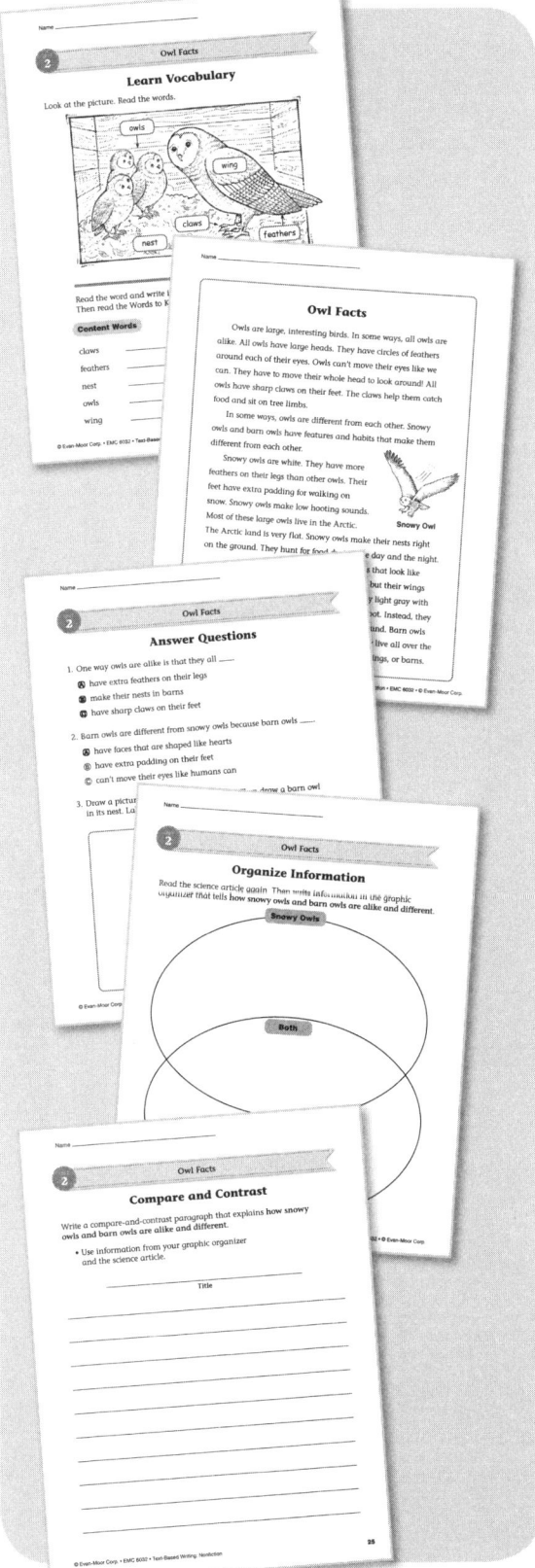

2 Learn Vocabulary

Direct students' attention to the picture dictionary. Read aloud each content vocabulary word and have students repeat. Point out that the words are related to owls and that students will have a better understanding of the words after they read the science article. Have students write the vocabulary words on the provided lines. Then review the Words to Know, and encourage students to ask questions about any words they do not understand.

3 Read the Science Article: *Owl Facts*

Read aloud the science article as students follow along silently. Then have students reread the article independently or in small groups.

4 Answer Questions About the Science Article

To ensure reading comprehension, have students answer the text-dependent questions. Review the answers together.

5 Organize Information

Explain to students that they will use a compare-and-contrast graphic organizer to help them plan their paragraphs. Guide students in using the text to complete the organizer, rereading the article if needed.

Remind students that a compare-and-contrast paragraph:

- tells how two or more things are alike, and
- tells how two or more things are different.

6 Write a Compare-and-Contrast Paragraph

Instruct students to complete the writing assignment independently, with a partner, or in small groups.

If needed, review the structure of a compare-and-contrast paragraph:

- The topic sentence tells about the two subjects.
- Details support the topic sentence and tell how the subjects are alike and different.

Name _____

UNIT 2

Owl Facts

Unit Focus

You are going to read a science article about snowy owls and barn owls.

As You Read:

Think about how these owls are alike and different.

After You Read:

Use information from the article to write a compare-and-contrast paragraph about the owls.

Lesson Checklist

Check off each task after you complete it.

- [ ] **Learn Vocabulary**
- [ ] **Read the Science Article:** *Owl Facts*
- [ ] **Answer Questions About the Science Article**
- [ ] **Organize Information**
- [ ] **Write a Compare-and-Contrast Paragraph**

Name _____

Owl Facts

Learn Vocabulary

Look at the picture. Read the words.

Read the word and write it on the line.
Then read the Words to Know.

Content Words

claws   _____
feathers _____
nest   _____
owls   _____
wing   _____

Words to Know

Arctic	hiss
eyes	hoot
habits	interesting
heads	screech

Name _____

Owl Facts

Owls are large, interesting birds. In some ways, all owls are alike. All owls have large heads. They have circles of feathers around each of their eyes. Owls can't move their eyes like we can. They have to move their whole head to look around! All owls have sharp claws on their feet. The claws help them catch food and sit on tree limbs.

In some ways, owls are different from each other. Snowy owls and barn owls have features and habits that make them different from each other.

Snowy owls are white. They have more feathers on their legs than other owls. Their feet have extra padding for walking on snow. Snowy owls make low hooting sounds. Most of these large owls live in the Arctic.

Snowy Owl

The Arctic land is very flat. Snowy owls make their nests right on the ground. They hunt for food during the day and the night.

Barn Owl

Barn owls have white faces that look like hearts. Their bodies are small, but their wings are large. Barn owls are usually light gray with some spots. Barn owls do not hoot. Instead, they make a hissing or screeching sound. Barn owls hunt for food only at night. They live all over the world. They make their nests in tree holes, buildings, or barns.

Name _____

Owl Facts

Answer Questions

1. One way owls are alike is that they all ____.

    Ⓐ have extra feathers on their legs

    Ⓑ make their nests in barns

    Ⓒ have sharp claws on their feet

2. Barn owls are different from snowy owls because barn owls ____.

    Ⓐ have faces that are shaped like hearts

    Ⓑ have extra padding on their feet

    Ⓒ can't move their eyes like humans can

3. Draw a picture of a snowy owl in its nest. Then draw a barn owl in its nest. Label each part of your pictures.

Name _____

Owl Facts

Organize Information

Read the science article again. Then write information in the graphic organizer that tells **how snowy owls and barn owls are alike and different**.

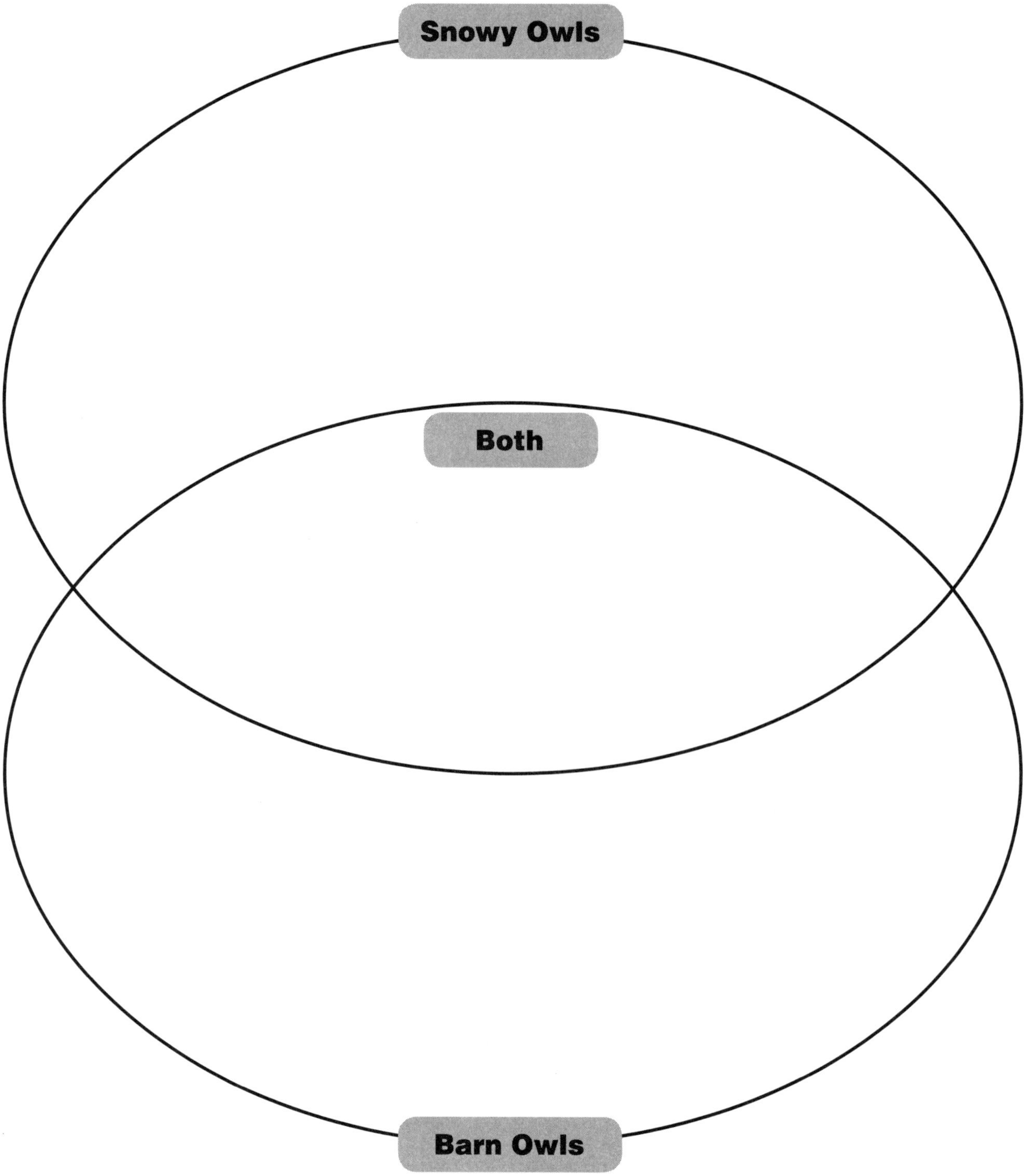

Snowy Owls

Both

Barn Owls

Name _____

Owl Facts

Compare and Contrast

Write a compare-and-contrast paragraph that explains **how snowy owls and barn owls are alike and different**.

- Use information from your graphic organizer and the science article.

_____
Title

_____
_____
_____
_____
_____
_____
_____
_____
_____
_____

© Evan-Moor Corp. • EMC 6032 • Text-Based Writing: Nonfiction